SMOOTH
FAILING

Top industry leaders share their
secrets for turning *pain* into **profit**.

Barbara Weltman

...words worth reading

/—

SMOOTH FAILING

Top industry leaders share their
secrets for turning *pain* into **profit**.

Barbara Weltman

List of Testimonials for

Smooth Failing

Voltaire once wrote "Common sense is not so common." What an understatement! Why do 90% of entrepreneurial business starts fail and 90% of all franchise business starts succeed? Simple: There are common sense rules for business success and franchisers have figured them out. And so has Barbara Weltman in her new book *Smooth Failing*. Starting a business? Avoid this book at your own peril. Buy and read this common sense book and dramatically increase your odds for success!

Kenneth W. Gronbach
Demographer and Futurist
President and CEO
KGC Direct, LLC

The stories in *Smooth Failing* remind me of our "worst idea" technique, where intentionally bad, ridiculous or even just plain stupid ideas are used to inspire great ones. By looking at the other side of success — difficult business failures and the lessons learned from them — Barbara Weltman's courageous authors have shined a bright light on thought-leading business practices.

Bryan Mattimore
Author, *21 Days to a Big Idea*

Contrary to the popular belief, there is no shame in failure.

Failure can be a great motivator. It can become a positive learning experience. To come back from failure is the sign of true grit.

But professional failure is often hidden…and that should not be. This is one of the many reasons why I found "Smooth Failing" such a rewarding and refreshing read. I appreciate the honesty of the featured entrepreneurs who generously share their often-fraught experiences. Author Barbara Weltman, who also shares her own challenges, has captured their stories in a captivating and an insightful manner.

I heartily recommend *"Smooth Failing"* to all entrepreneurs – or any person in business – as a must-read.

Jennefer Witter
CEO/Founder, The Boreland Group

Barbara Weltman has done the undoable. She has put together a compendium of uncommon wisdom from some of the most brilliant business minds of our time, yet instead of asking them to convey their sage advice, she gets them to reveal their most critical mistakes. As a person that has saved thousands of businesses, I am all too familiar with the myriad of mistakes business owners make and Barbara's clear and concise style enables the reader to easily benefit from the humility of the most successful.

Jerry Silberman
CEO & Founder, Corporate Turnaround

Barbara Weltman pulls back the curtain to show how successful business owners have had to struggle to achieve success. In relating their stories, Barbara explains how you can put their lessons to use and avoid costly mistakes in your own business. The stories are not just entertaining but inspire readers to think in new ways and turn challenges into triumphs.

Ina Steiner
Editor and co-founder, eCommerceBytes.com

If you are an entrepreneur, you will fail at some point. Whether you will succeed overall depends on how you handle those setbacks. *Smooth Failing* offers practical, proven strategies for navigating common challenges. A thoroughly enjoyable and informative read.

Gerri Detweiler
Education Editor for Nav and
Co-author of *Finance Your Own Business*

Smooth Failing is practical and to the point insights in how to succeed in your business. Great insights from a strong cast of business owners and experts in business.

Ramon Ray
Founder
Smart Hustle Magazine and SmallBizTechnology.com

Foreword for Smooth Failing

by
Jim Blasingame

Host of The Small Business Advocate Show
Author of *The 3rd Ingredient* –

The Journey of Analog Ethics into the World
of Digital Fear and Greed

In my reading over the years, I've consistently been drawn to autobiographies of people who took great risks and found greater success. Of course, you can't go wrong reading about the great intellects and leaders like Washington, Lincoln, Churchill, etc. But my favorite autobiographies have been those who are/were alive during my life, because I could identify with the issues they were up against.

Contemplating why I've been drawn to this genre, eventually I realized it wasn't because I was in awe of their celebrity, or riches, or other success markers. It was because in every honest autobiography there is a heaping helping of examples of how that person failed. Modern failures.

Why do I love that part of their personal stories? Because they admitted they were human. They fessed up to examples of when they were bone-headed, or egomaniacal, or just plain stupid. That's why I like my good friend Barbara Weltman's book, *Smooth Failing,* which is full of such stories.

One of the things I get to do in my job – now for more than 20 years – is interview accomplished people on my radio program, like the autobiographers I mentioned. Sure, I let them tell my audience about spiking the ball in the end zone of the marketplace. But I also ask about the times when they fumbled the ball away, allowing the other team to win the game. And you know what? Everyone has had more than one story to tell, and not one has ever refused to reveal their bone-head story. Not one. That kind of honest leadership is found throughout Barbara's book.

It's true, you learn more from failures than you do from successes. The reason, I think, is because when you succeed you're not inclined to be introspective – obviously you won because you were so smart. When's the party, right? But when you miss a sale, blow a deal, lose a customer, or as I have done, lock the doors one last time on a failing business, the absence of a victory party allows you time for precious introspection. In *Smooth Failing,* Barbara's contributors share their relationship with this kind of introspection.

Introspection after a failure is precious is because it shines a light on your investment in what Edison called, "successfully discovering what doesn't work." Without introspection, you could be in jeopardy of discovering my father's farm wisdom: "There's no education in the second kick of a mule." In fact, the case could be made for also celebrating failure. How valuable is knowing the better path to take whether you're calling on the next customer or reloading and reinventing your career? I know most of Barbara's interviewees in this book, and I'm pretty sure they've all thrown a failure party at some point in time, even if there was only one partier.

When a successful person has limited time and can either tell you how smart they are, or how stupid they once were, take the latter. In that spirit, with all the excellent books available to show you how to succeed, *Smooth Failing* will show you how human it is to come up short, and the precious future success currency that can be acquired from that experience.

Of course, no one wants to fail. But since, as a human, that isn't one of our options, the goal should be to develop a healthy relationship with failure, so when the inevitable happens, we can turn it into an investment, not an expense.

Thanks, Barbara, for having the courage to make available such an important book on wise investing.

Smooth Failing

Introduction

Bobby Jones, an amateur golfer who won the Grand Slam of golf and started Augusta National (where the Masters Tournament is held annually), said, "I never learned anything from a tournament I won." Failure is a great teacher. It makes us stop and think why things went wrong, how things could have been done differently, and how they can be done correctly in the future. Bottom line: failure isn't a waste of time.

In a perfect world, an entrepreneur with a great business idea would start up and go from one success to another. But this isn't a perfect world, and the road to success is paved with failures. These failures produce pain, humiliation, anxiety, financial loss, and frustration. But they also result in personal growth and business progress . . . as long as you know how to handle errors, mistakes, and failures.

Several years ago, *Psychology Today* had a useful article about recovering from failure. It contained a lot of tips including keeping a sense of humor, not blaming everything on yourself (or on others), and seeing failure as the gateway to opportunity. These are great ideas to keep in mind about failure in general. But these psychology-oriented ideas for recovering from failure may not be specific enough to help business owners and those who would like to be in business.

Some time ago, my fortune in the fortune cookie from a Chinese restaurant read, "Mistakes show us what we need to learn." That got me thinking about failure and writing this book. When I think about failure, I simultaneously think about success. Perhaps it's because I put a face to the words, and that face is of Abraham Lincoln. He was, perhaps, the most successful President that the United States of America has ever had. He saved the United States, abolished slavery, and spoke some of the most memorable words in U. S. history including the Gettysburg address. Survey after survey on the presidents puts him at the very top or near to it. I'd call that success. But history shows that he is a case study in failure. How's this for failure?

- He was defeated for State Legislator in 1832.
- He started a business only to see it go under. It was a store in New Salem, Illinois. His partner died, and he could not sustain the business. He eventually paid off all of the business' debts.
- He lost his run for Congress in 1843 and again in 1848.
- He lost his bid to become a U. S. Senator in 1855.
- He ran for Vice President of the U. S. in 1856 and lost.

- He again ran for the U. S. Senate in 1859 and lost yet again.

These failures did not keep him from running for president and winning the following year. In addition, sprinkled among his failures was the creation of a very successful law practice as well as a number of *successful* election campaigns.

President Lincoln is a role model—at least for me. He aimed high and often failed, but he also succeeded on a grand scale. That's what I think most entrepreneurs would like for themselves.

It's not necessary for you to experience failure in order to avoid problems; instead, it's *better*—and certainly less painful—to learn about the failures of others in business so that you can hopefully avoid similar failure in your own endeavors. I believe this whole-heartedly, so I've reached out to several highly successful small business people to share the lessons they've learned from their failures. These individuals have been a part of important and creative businesses or organizations, and they have graciously shared their personal—and often unflattering—experiences in their lives.

I also confess to a number of failures on the road to what I consider a successful and long career, so I also share my experiences. I hope, after reading these compelling stories, that you'll be freed from the fear of failure and have the courage to continue to strive for excellence in business while also having the wisdom to avoid some of the problems shared in this book.

—*Barbara Weltman*

Lesson

Don't Mistake Activity for Effective Action

Anita Campbell

Founder and CEO of Small Business Trends, LLC

> *"A goal without a plan is just a wish."*
> —Antoine de Saint-Exupéry

For the most part, entrepreneurs are goal-oriented. Whether it's achieving a targeted number for annual revenue, bringing a new product to market by a set date, or opening a second or tenth location, we're used to setting short-term and long-term goals for both our businesses and ourselves. When I begin teaching my class in entrepreneurship every semester, I ask the students: "How do you define success for yourself?" If they can't articulate this, how will they know whether they've achieved it? Is success making a certain amount of money? Gaining fame? Supporting a family? Helping the community? Changing the world?

In order to succeed, you have to know what success means to you personally, keep that goal in mind, and make a plan designed to achieve it. Of course, even when you've clarified *exactly* what it is you want, staying focused on your long-term objectives isn't always easy once the hard work, minutia, and day-to-day tasks begin.

As John Lennon said, "Life is what happens while you're busy making other plans." Even if we have clear objectives and a good business plan, we don't necessarily proceed in the right direction. When we get off track, we often figure that if we just work hard, or harder, we'll achieve our goals. We're so hard at work that we fail to monitor whether we are moving any closer to those goals.

At least that's what happened to Anita Campbell. After a successful career as a corporate attorney and executive, in 2003 she founded Small Business Trends (https://smallbiztrends. com), an online information portal for the small business community providing news, tips, and advice. More than 6 million small businesses, including mine, get information from her site annually. She soon founded several other sites, each of which played off the original. She became busy doing much of the writing for her sites, as well as for other media outlets. Anita became a much sought-after speaker and a well-known figure as a small business expert. Her calendar was full, and she was profitable.

But year after year, she wasn't moving any closer to her ultimate goal—to build a website entity so powerful that it could eventually be sold for millions. Her central site and its sister sites were up and running, but they weren't growing as she had hoped. She'd seen other sites, many of which started after hers, that were sold for millions of dollars. Tech Crunch, which was launched in 2006 and acquired by AOL in 2010, fetched a reported $25 million; Mashable, which was launched in 2005, was in talks as of August 2012 to be acquired by CNN for reportedly more than $200 million; and the Huffington Post, which launched in 2005, was acquired by AOL in 2011 for $315 million. Her sites weren't growing in the way they needed to if they were ever to become a buyout target.

Most mistakes that business owners make blow up in their faces like bombs. The detonation brings down the house (and maybe the business), forcing owners to re-evaluate their situation and plot revised strategies. That didn't happen to Anita. There was no sudden or dramatic event that brought her world to a stand-still. Instead, in late 2010, she had an epiphany.

Anita realized that she was simply in a fog and on autopilot when it came to running her business. She had to shake off the lethargy she was in and face the fact that she was not doing what was needed to move her closer to her goal. She felt like she'd been asleep for a long time and was waking up from a dream. A light had just been turned on, and she could see things more clearly now. From a personal perspective, she felt disappointed and frustrated with herself. She had wasted years on worthy activities, but they failed to move her any closer to her goals. She had spread herself too thin and had lost her focus.

From a business perspective, the epiphany was just what was needed to get her moving. Anita realized that she could no longer run the business as a solo entrepreneur. To achieve her goal, she had to think and act differently. She had to implement targeted activities. She needed to create a business organization that could operate independently from her personal efforts; only such an organization could eventually be sold for megabucks. For the first time, she hired a full-time IT manager, and her website traffic doubled within the first year.

Anita also realized that she had to spend her time differently. She couldn't devote it to writing and speaking—

these were worthy activities that furthered her personal brand, but they did not move her toward her goal. She had to spend her hours working on her business. Anita couldn't maintain the number of different websites that she was trying to run simultaneously; she had to make cuts so that her time could be used more effectively in a targeted manner.

By taking the steps above, Anita dramatically increased her web traffic while streamlining and strengthening her company's brand. That growth continues as of this publication, and Small Business Trends is steadily moving into position for a sizable buyout.

Looking back on the years she spent in a diverse range of activities that were not effective movers toward her goals, Anita recognizes that it's too easy for any entrepreneur to fall into the same trap. Opportunities present themselves and they are seductively appealing—they provide money, fame, and the appearance of success. But you have to move out of your comfort zone and into the areas of work that will move you forward.

Anita's Lessons

- *Keep your goals in sight.* Don't get lost in the everyday pulls of running a business and forget your goals. To paraphrase Michael Gerber, author of The *E-Myth Revisited,* you must work on your business, not just *in* it.

- *Find trusted people to work with.* You can't move forward without help from others. Be sure that the people you choose to work with, whether as partners, employees, or associates, are capable of delivering the work you expect from them and are the type of individuals with the integrity you can rely on.

Like Anita, I have goals for my business. I closed my law practice in 2004 to work full-time on my information services business. My vision statement for my business was "To provide accurate and helpful information that small business owners can use to save time and money, stay out of trouble, and boost the bottom line." I eventually reduced my vision statement to a mantra: "To make entrepreneurs smarter." I wanted to provide solid, usable information that both potential and seasoned entrepreneurs could use in their businesses. This business was my second act too; but unlike Anita, I wasn't looking to create a multimillion dollar company. I just wanted to grow my audience and put the information out there while making a living.

However, like Anita, over time I realized that I too was spreading myself too thin and losing focus in pursuing my goal. I was trying to do everything myself. I tried to manage not only the writing, speaking, teaching, hosting of a radio show, and other core activities of my business, but also all of the administrative chores. I was the booking agent, content editor, bookkeeper, IT expert, and producer. If I'd let myself, I could have worked 24/7 because I had that much to do.

It eventually became apparent to me that I needed help. Like Anita, this realization wasn't the result of a bomb going off in my business. It was simply a lightbulb that came on. I was having coffee one day with a colleague, and she mentioned that she used a virtual assistant to help arrange her speaking engagements. I learned from her about virtual assistants, who, in the old days would have been called executive secretaries. Virtual assistants have their own businesses, and as a rule, do not work fulltime with any one client. With the Internet, a business owner can use such a professional, who can be located just about anywhere. My colleague had found a virtual assistant through a site called AssistU (https://www.assistu. com), so I posted my needs there and interviewed about a dozen applicants who responded to my post. I immediately eliminated those who were more than one time zone away from me (My preference is to work in closer proximity with someone.). I found a perfect match—someone who could edit my blogs, articles, and other writings, produce my radio show, handle my social media, and take care of just about anything else that would arise.

I also engaged a bookkeeper to handle my QuickBooks and an IT company to monitor my site and be on-call for website emergencies. And I use professionals for various other purposes: copyediting, ongoing website development, and more. I have also enlisted my retired husband to help me with odds and ends including photocopying, trips to the post office, and, yes, getting me coffee. It's a plus for me, and it gets him off the couch (which is a plus for him)!

The cost of this help isn't cheap (You get what you pay for.), but it is worth every penny. To put things in perspective, if I can bill out $500 an hour for the work I do and I pay an assistant $35 to $75 an hour or more (depending on the type of assistant), I'm obviously ahead of the game. But even better, getting help enables me to devote my time to doing what I love to do which is the writing, speaking, and teaching. It frees me from administrative chores that take time but are not rewarding to me.

Barbara's Lessons

- *Don't do it all yourself.* While you retain responsibility for every aspect of your company, you don't have to personally handle every business chore.

- *Build the cost of good help into your budget.* You want to engage the most qualified people you can to help your business. This costs money. Be prepared to pay for the best people you can.

Anita Campbell

Anita is the Founder, CEO, and Editor-in-Chief of Small Business Trends LLC in Medina, Ohio. Before starting her company, she was the Senior Vice President of Bell & Howell Publishing Services, culminating in the role of CEO  of an information technology subsidiary of Bell & Howell. Prior to that, she was an executive and associate counsel for a regional bank. Besides running her company, she serves on various boards including as Vice Chair of the Advisory Board for the Center for Information Technology and eBusiness at the University of Akron, and advisory boards for several companies that sell to the small business market. She's the co-author of Visual Marketing: *99 Proven Ways for Small Businesses to Market with Images and Design.*

Lesson

Make Sure Your Goals Align with Those of Your Investors

Gary Hoover

Serial Entrepreneur

> *"You may win the battle but lose the war."*
> —Derived from Sun Tzu's *The Art of War*

Entrepreneurs love to start businesses; that's what they do. However, in order to grow the business, they have to learn to let go. Doug and Polly White, authors of *Let Go to Grow*, describe three stages of a business: a micro-business when the founder does it all, a small business when employees are brought on board to handle many tasks that the founder had previously done, and a mid-size business when managers are needed to oversee employees. The book, however, does not go on to the next phase: big business.

In order to become big, most companies need outside financing. Loans won't cut it, so investors become essential. For investments up to about $500,000 or $1 million, angels or angel groups can be tapped. Angels come in all shapes and sizes, although typically they are individuals who are well-educated, have business experience, and are modestly wealthy. In exchange for their capital, they receive an ownership interest; they usually don't participate in any business activities and may or may not provide any business advice for the company.

Once a business needs more money, venture capitalists may be the solution. These are firms seeking to underwrite high-potential companies (2,749 companies received venture capital in 2010 in the U.S.). For their risk, venture capitalists take a measure of ownership; they may also provide guidance on or even dictate how the company is run. And, most importantly, they expect to reap substantial financial rewards in a relatively short period of time (usually less than five years).

An entrepreneur may not be able to achieve his or her dream of creating a successful big business without the help of venture capital, but there can be a steep price to pay for this funding. Gary followed the steps to creating a big company and signed a deal with investors that gave them the right to change management—all while keeping his "eyes wide open."

It seems that Gary was born to be in business and had a strong background for success. At 12 years old, he subscribed to *Fortune* magazine. At the University of Chicago, he studied economics under Nobel Prize winners George Stigler, Robert Fogel, and Milton Friedman. In his first jobs on Wall Street and in retailing, he achieved recognition and success and developed the burning desire to create his own successful enterprise. With this strong business background under his belt, in March 1982, he founded BOOKSTOP, a book superstore, and opened his first store that September.

While the first and second stores were financed by angel investors (private individuals who took equity in exchange for their cash), when the next four stores opened with capital from a strategic partner (corporate investor), Gary then realized venture capital money would be needed to continue the rapid growth. There was no stopping Gary; and in a few years, he was able to secure venture capital, which he used to grow BOOKSTOP from 6 stores to 12 stores in just one year! BOOKSTOP was now the first chain of book superstores.

Gary was feeling pretty good about himself. He had accomplished something unique, creating a chain of book superstores. He enjoyed being around the books and customers, and whenever he had a low moment, he'd visit the various stores and wait on customers, which would recharge his spirit. He was looking forward to continued expansion and enjoying his work with the bookstores for years to come. But then the bomb dropped.

Gary scheduled the next board meeting and planned to meet with investors in a hotel near the airport, a convenient meeting place because some of them had to fly in for the meeting. He expected that they would discuss what was happening in the company, what changes might be needed, and goals for the next quarters. The company hadn't made a profit and, in fact, lost more money than they expected. Gary recognized that one of the problems was inventory control, but he felt he was on it (technology in 1989 had not yet provided canned software for inventory control so Gary wrote the company's first program for this purpose). Indeed, the investors did want to talk about change, but the change they had in mind was Gary. He was fired on the spot.

He was blindsided—something he now attributes to his own inexperience and youthful optimism—and never saw this as a possible scenario in the meeting. The investors felt that as a result of the company's recent failures, some heads should roll. Gary defended his team—to the extent that when the investors wanted heads to roll, he implied, "If you want to get rid of them, you'll have to get rid of me." So they said, "Goodbye." They had come prepared and had already hired a successor. He was in shock. That night, as he walked the floor of his hotel room, he could not immediately process what had just happened. BOOKSTOP was his baby. Gary had hired the company's 600 employees with whom he continued to feel an emotional connection. He now had to go back to his headquarters and introduce his successor.

Personally, the firing was devastating. While he had a financial backstop because he continued to hold his shares in BOOKSTOP, he still felt the loss. Ultimately, he recognized that the investors were counting on the results that he had projected; and as CEO, he was responsible for the company's performance. Gary, too, wanted to build a company of great value as quickly as possible. He wanted to spend the rest of his life at BOOKSTOP and proceeded to manage the company with this in mind; they wanted to cash out as quickly as possible and Gary wasn't taking the actions they thought were needed to meet their goal.

In 1989, a few months after his firing while serving as a member of the board, and just seven years from the inception of BOOKSTOP, the company was sold to Barnes & Noble for $41.5 million. The venture capitalists had tripled their money in 18 months. Gary, however, was only a minority owner by this time. His original 30% ownership share had been diluted because of the introduction of new investors to just 6%. Still, this was not a bad payday for him.

Gary went on to found another successful company, the Reference Press, which morphed into Hoover's, Inc., a business information services firm which he started in 1990.

The firm provided company profiles for businesses interested in B2B activities. The company went public in 1999, but he remained a board member until it was bought out by Dun & Bradstreet in 2003. Other companies followed, and he has recently incorporated his fifth startup. Today, Gary spends his time imparting his vast knowledge with others. He lectures around the world to both CEOs and schoolchildren, sharing his passion for entrepreneurship.

Gary's Lessons

- *Take the task of raising capital seriously.* It's a catch-22; it can be difficult and slow to build a big business without outside equity capital, but you want investors with goals that are congruent with yours.

  For example, if your goal is long-term, be sure that investors plan to stay for the long term rather than cashing out quickly. Communication up front can go a long way toward a satisfactory coexistence with outside investors.

- *Keep your eyes open wide with respect to investors.*
  Once you take outside money, everything changes in the business. They may be working something completely different unless you continue to communicate. Be sure to continue your dialogue and continually revisit your common goals.

- *Listen to your board and other outsiders, and take their comments seriously.* Listen to others and know when to back off positions you have maintained. With outside investors, you'll have to give ground. Recognize this fact so it doesn't eat you up.

While I've never taken outside money for Big Ideas for Small Business, Inc., I've been involved with other firms that have sought venture capital. One company I'm currently working with is DynaTax (I'm a 2% owner.), which owns several patents and is developing more that we hope to translate into helpful and profitable tax planning tools. The patent process is expensive as is the programming needed to make the concepts commercially viable, so we needed outside financing. This isn't easy to come by, and we turned to people we know for money. Family and friends are historically the first option for starting a business (The SBA reports that 36% of startup equity is from owners' savings and investments from family and friends.). Family and friends are often good resources for additional financing to grow a business.

DynaTax's founder, Gary Abeles, turned to his good friend who I'll call Sam. Gary decided that the company needed both money and an investor who could direct the company into revenue streams. Gary knew Sam well and was aware of Sam's successes in the past with various businesses. Sam had many good ideas on how his investment in the company could be utilized to generate revenue. Unfortunately, the money came, but the actions to generate revenue did not. Months passed, but the company was no closer to market than before Sam became an investor. Our goals did not align with those of our investor. We were ready and eager to move the business forward quickly; Sam did nothing to further this goal for an entire year.

The problem now is how to continue to be in business with Sam. His ownership cannot be undone merely because he failed to come through on his promises to promote the business. And now, a friendship of many years is likely to end. Gary and I recognize that, in the future, raising money from friends may not be the best answer for DynaTax. We've learned a hard lesson that taking the easy road to outside financing by tapping friends is not the best course in the long run.

Barbara's Lessons

- *Be wary of financing from friends and family.* While having investors you know has advantages, such as a level of trust that is not always present with strangers and the ability to get the money quickly, there are drawbacks to consider. The chief disadvantage is that when the business goes bad, relationships sour. It's not easy sitting down to Thanksgiving dinner with family members who have lost their investments in your now-defunct business.

- *Grasp the financial realities of selling ownership interests.* My dad, who brought in angel investors to his company to help it survive and grow, told me it's better to own a small percentage of something than 100% of nothing.

But don't be quick to give away too much. It's important to strike a balance between full ownership and becoming a minority owner of the company you created.

- *Be realistic.* The adage that you can't get something for nothing applies to venture capitalism. You have to give away absolute control in order to get the money you need to take your business to the next level. The percentage of ownership you need to part with depends on how much money you're getting and how desperate you are for the funding.

Gary Hoover

A serial entrepreneur, Gary has founded five companies including BOOKSTOP (which was purchased by Barnes & Noble), Hoover's Inc., a busi- ness information services firm (which went public and was purchased by Dun & Bradstreet), two businesses which changed industries, and another in its early startup phase. In 2009–10, Gary served as Entrepreneur-in-Residence at the McCombs School of Business at the University of Texas in Austin; and in 2012–13, he served as the Entrepreneur-in-Residence at the UT School of Information. He continues to be a student of business and speak to audiences around the world about what he believes are the eight keys to creating, building, and leading successful enterprises. Today, he blogs and video blogs—see www.hooversworld.com.

Lesson

Don't Lie to
Customers and Clients

Gene Marks

CEO of The Marks Group, PC

"It is better to offer no excuse than a bad one."

—George Washington

In New York City's Diamond District, located on 47th Street between Fifth and Sixth Avenues, there are 2,600 independent businesses that conduct an estimated $400 million in revenue a day. Business between Hasidic Jewish merchants on the block is done with a traditional blessing and a handshake. There are no written contracts, only oral agreements. These informal transactions work because each party relies on the fact that the other is honest and trustworthy. If one party proves to be dishonest, he will never work again in the diamond industry. His bad name will travel through the ranks faster than salacious details in a celebrity's Twitter account.

When talking about honesty in the context of business relations, there's always a question about whether this means complete and total disclosure. Is it deceitful to keep certain facts secret? Is it lying to flatter customers and clients who don't deserve it? I leave it for you to decide. But one thing I think we can agree on is that, "Honesty," as Shakespeare said, "is the best policy." That's something Gene Marks learned the hard way.

Gene, who is a CPA by trade, left KPMG, a national accounting firm, after eight years to join his dad in business. In 1994, he started doing part-time service implementation for accounting software developed by his dad, who also handled sales. At the same time, Gene was the controller for a public company in the biotech industry (It has since gone out of business.). After a couple of years as a controller, he left to work full-time with his dad. One of the problems Gene encountered in doing so was that the software was flawed. To be fair, accounting software at that time was in its infancy, and his company's product was effective in recording income and expenses.

The main flaw in the software was that it couldn't generate financial statements. This meant that Gene had to work with customers to help create the financial statements using spreadsheets. All of this work on Gene's part to keep customers satisfied (and compete with other software products like QuickBooks) took a great deal of time and ate into the company's cash flow. But what else could he do? He couldn't think of anything at the time.

One client, who I'll call Joe, owned a manufacturing company in Pennsylvania, and Joe was a stickler for details. He wanted certain financials, including a job-costing report, and Gene was glad to oblige. Unfortunately, because of limited time and resources, Gene was unable to generate the type of financials that lived up to the client's expectations. He thought the client wouldn't notice, but he did. Joe called him on this, and what was Gene's reaction? He lied. Back then, Gene thought that close enough was good enough. He claimed the financials were correct, even though he knew there were problems that could have been corrected if given more time.

This lie led him to more deceit. Like Bill Clinton when asked about having had sexual relations with Monica

Lewinsky, Gene not only lied about it, but also denied the fact that he lied. Because he knew he'd done wrong, he then failed to take Joe's phone calls.

All the while, this whole event started to take a physical toll on him. He became sick to his stomach and couldn't shake the bad feelings about himself. And he realized after the fact that he spent more time lying, dodging, and making excuses than if he'd just owned up to the mistake and corrected it.

From a business perspective, as you might have guessed, he lost the client. At that time, the business was struggling, he had young children, and the loss of any client was significant to him. He also had to tell his father, his business partner, what really caused the loss of the client.

In 2000, Gene's company's software product was rendered obsolete because it had not been programmed for the new millennium (This error was referred to at the time as the Y2K glitch.), forcing Gene's business to take a different turn. His company became software resellers, which they continue to be today. Once the software became obsolete, he was relieved of having to personally generate financials for customers, something he didn't like to do.

As a result of this experience, Gene was reborn about honesty. He learned to recognize the importance of being honest to customers, clients, employees, vendors, and other business associates. He doesn't like to deal with anyone who he suspects of dishonesty. And he believes he is a better person and a better business owner for the experience.

The experience helped him to grow as a person and as a business owner. Today, he not only runs a successful sales and marketing technology firm, but has also become a respected voice of small business. He provides advice through his columns, top-selling books, and media appearances, and is followed by more than 68,000 viewers on Twitter.

Gene's Lessons

- *Establish credibility by being honest.* Customers like to do business with people they trust. Customers will make referrals only to people they like doing business with. So, being honest leads to customers which leads to referrals.

- *Own up to your mistakes.* Mistakes are inevitable. Just admit your fault, correct it (even if it costs the business money), and move on.

Like everyone else, I make mistakes. Mine, however, are often very visible because they appear in print or online. I've been writing about taxes and business issues for more than 35 years. My writings have appeared in major publications such as the *Wall Street Journal and U.S. News and World Reports.* I've written over 100 books, taking into account annual revisions of various titles. I've provided content for the U.S. Small Business Administration, American Express OPEN Forum, JKLasser.com, as well as many Fortune 500 companies for which my name is not seen.

So if I write something that has an error in it, thousands of people may see it. Some may even rely on it and experience problems later on. I know that I have a great responsibility when I write anything other than opinion pieces.

As much as I try to be accurate in everything I write, mistakes happen. For example, with the tax material I write about, there are always numbers and dates, and it's all too easy to slip up from time to time, indicating a wrong year or dropping a digit on a tax limitation.

When I discover an error or have one brought to my attention by a reader, like Gene, it gives me a bad feeling in my stomach. However, I've learned to follow Bruce Lee's advice: "Mistakes are always forgivable, if one has the courage to admit them." I embrace the term "erratum" to remind readers of an error and to correct the information. My annual book *J.K. Lasser's Small Business Taxes,* comes out in the fall; and I almost always inevitably discover an error or two after a book has gone to print. Fortunately, there is an online supplement posted on my site and on JKLasser.com, where I can list any errors in the book.

Of course, it's always better to not have errors in the first place. To avoid any errors up front, I try to have as many pairs of eyes as possible look over my work before it goes public. A typo can be a significant error and something that can be easily detected by having other people review my work. A minor mistake can appear large and damage my reputation for reliability and accuracy, so I take this very seriously.

Barbara's Lessons

- *Correct mistakes.* Take the time to point out mistakes even if customers and clients don't realize you made them. This will enhance your credibility.

- *Plan for review.* Use others—whether it's employees, contractors, or in my case, my husband—to look over work before it's shared with the public.

Gene Marks

Gene owns and operates The Marks Group PC, a 10-person firm in Bala Cynwyd, PA (outside of Philadelphia) that provides sales and marketing technology and consulting services to small and medium-sized businesses. The Marks Group PC, launched in 1994, has grown to help more than 600 companies and thousands of individuals throughout the country. Gene is also a columnist, author, and media personality, with his articles appearing in *The New York Times, Forbes* magazine, and the *Huffington Post.* His most recent book is *God We Trust, Everyone Else Pays Cash—Simple Lessons from Smart Business People.*

Lesson

Do Your Due Diligence in Vetting Clients, and Don't Be Surprised by Anything

John Jantsch

Founder and CEO of Duct Tape Marketing

> *"There are three things that cannot long be hidden: the sun, the moon, and the truth."*
>
> —Buddha

One of the great things about being in business is that you never know what's going to happen in the course of the day. I've never been bored a single day since I became involved in business, in part because of that anticipation of what's around the corner. What new project or opportunity will fall in my lap? Unfortunately, what's around the corner isn't always good. The next thing I know, the power goes out, and my business with it for the time being. A customer goes under, and my bill goes unpaid. After doing considerable upfront work, the contract I expected to get never materializes. Oh well.

Perhaps even more exciting than what can happen is the possibility of who you're going to meet today. A casual hello while waiting in line for morning coffee can lead to a new client, a great referral, or even a lasting relationship.

The flip side, of course, is the possibility of meeting someone who isn't so nice or, even worse, who isn't what he or she seems to be. Or perhaps you land a client who gives you an uneasy "gut feeling," but you can't put your finger on why, and you feel you can't afford to be picky. After all, they're willing to pay, right?

Maybe you can never really know who a person is, as John Jantsch's experience demonstrates. He started his marketing company, Jantsch Communications, in 1983 as a traditional marketing agency. After a while, he was doing small projects with a number of large organizations and had a respectable list of clients. Fast forward a number of years, and John was doing well; but he wasn't enjoying himself. He was no longer excited about his company or his clients—working with large businesses wasn't fun for him. There was one huge company in particular that John never felt completely comfortable with, but it was a client he'd done business with for years. It was one of his top five accounts, and it contributed significantly to his company's revenue. All in all, he wasn't happy, but he plodded on.

In addition to the large organizations that John dealt with, he had also acquired a number of small business clients, most of whom he liked, trusted, and really enjoyed working with. Unfortunately, he couldn't make a living on their accounts; their projects were small and the money was too. Because the level of service required and the paperwork involved for the small accounts was just not worth it, John didn't actively pursue new small business clients. Most of his focus remained on servicing larger organizations. That is, until one day in September 2001 when the FBI knocked at his door.

The FBI was investigating the very client that John never felt comfortable with. They were checking into the client's activities involving fraud and money laundering, and the agents wanted to know whether John, and anyone else the client had been doing business with, were involved in these illegal activities. Of course he wasn't, and he was promptly cleared of any wrongdoing. Also, he didn't have any knowledge of the client's illegal activities.

Still, this event was seismic to John and to his business. He was personally stunned to learn the truth about the client he had been working with for years. He felt betrayed and vulnerable. From a business perspective, the event proved to be too much to handle. John had to devote significant time to preparing for and testifying before a grand jury that eventually indicted his former client. Because this event coincided with the economic downturn following the events of 9/11, he also lost a number of important clients who could no longer budget for his services. This one-two punch forced John to stop what he had been doing and reassess.

At the end of 2001, just three months from the time of the knock on the door, he shut down his company, laid off his staff, and said goodbye to his remaining clients. He needed time to think about the direction he wanted to take, and he couldn't do it and run a company at the same time. He had some soul searching to do. And he followed Lucille Ball's quip that, "It's a helluva start, being able to recognize what makes you happy."

A little more than one month later, John was ready to re-launch his business, but in a whole new and improved direction. He remembered how much he enjoyed working with small businesses and how rewarding it felt to be of help to them. He found just the answer he had been searching for. In February 2002, John started Duct Tape Marketing, a company that provided a marketing system for small businesses based on the simple idea that marketing is nothing more than "getting people who have a specific need or problem to know, like, trust, do business with, *and* refer you to others who have the same need or problem." The name for the company is derived from the simple product, duct tape, which is incredibly powerful, very practical, and sticks where it is applied. With this new system, he could approach a small-business owner, tell her exactly what he was going to do for her company, exactly what to expect from his marketing help in terms of results, and exactly what it was going to cost. Sounds simple, but it was a unique and much-needed service at the time.

Seemingly overnight, his new business took off. John rapidly garnered national attention and soon wrote his first best-selling book entitled *Duct Tape Marketing*. He became the go-to guy for small business marketing, and today he is constantly in demand by reporters, media outlets, and others seeking his expertise. He parlayed the Internet into a launch pad for his ideas, accumulating over 100,000 subscribers for his blog. Now, his Duct Tape Marketing system is licensed around the world. He devotes much of his time to coaching, publishing, speaking, and developing new business projects.

Looking back, John admits he had a sixth sense that something wasn't right with the client. He never enjoyed working with the people there, but he ignored his gut feeling. As John admitted, he was in startup mode at the time he took on the client and was happy to take any business he could get. Now, he's in command and works only with people and businesses he likes and trusts.

John's Lessons

- *Don't try to rationalize away a bad feeling.* If you get bad vibes from a customer, don't discount them, even if the money seems good.

- *Do what you love.* If John had found a way with his old company to work with the small business owners he enjoyed getting to know on a personal basis, rather than the large companies that were in some ways unknowable, he would never have been hit by the labyrinthine mess connected to the lawless big client.

- *Don't take shortcuts.* Take the time to check things out and do things right to avoid problems later on. Maybe you won't uncover the fact that a client has a nefarious background or agenda, but maybe you will.

Like John, I was very surprised to learn the unsavory side of a person I had done business with for nearly 10 years. He owned the local IT company that serviced my computer. I socialized with him over the years at various networking events. He gave me tickets each year for my husband and me to attend minor league baseball games. One day, out of the blue, I got a phone call from another IT company telling me it acquired my old IT company and that it would be doing my servicing from now on. I didn't think much about it except maybe that the owner I knew was retiring or his company was merging to become a larger firm. From my perspective, I had a new service number and was covered for my needs. When the first bill from the new IT company arrived, I called the billing department to set up automatic payments. Casually, I inquired about the owner of the former company and the response was, "Didn't you know? Just Google his name." I did this, only to learn that he had been caught in a sting operation and was arrested for soliciting sex from a minor. (He hasn't been tried or convicted of anything yet.) This news came as a shock to me! The nice person I knew, or thought I knew, may very well be someone completely different. Can you ever prepare for this kind of rude awakening?

Barbara's Lessons

- *Don't be surprised by anything.* Whatever you think is true may not be true. This goes for people, companies, and products. Some may astound you because they are so good, while others may also astound you, but for the opposite reason—because they're so bad.

- *Be ready at any time to start over.* John remade his company to fit his new vision for better serving the small business community. I have a new IT company to get to know so I can work with them. Change happens. One of my favorite greeting cards is a picture of a dinner roll next to two punch bowls, with the caption: Roll with the punches.

John Jantsch

John is the CEO of Duct Tape Marketing and best-selling author of *Duct Tape Marketing: The World's Most Practical Small Business Marketing Guide,* which is now in its second edition. He is the creator of the Duct Tape Marketing System and Duct Tape Marketing Consulting Network that trains and licenses small business marketing consultants around the world. His blog is a "must-read," and he's had world acclaim for his insights and contributions to marketing for small businesses. https://www.ducttapemarketing.com/

Lesson

Determine Your Brand

Karen Kerrigan

Founder and CEO of the Small Business &
Entrepreneurship Council

> *"A brand is a living entity–and it is enriched
> or undermined cumulatively over time . . . the
> product of a thousand small gestures."*
>
> —Michael Eisner, former CEO
> of The Walt Disney Company

Business owners know the value of branding. It's what we strive to create so we can connect with our customers on a visceral level. When you see the Nike swoosh, the red Coca-Cola script, or IBM's big blue, immediately you connect the brand message of these companies. It takes time to create brand recognition and requires continual attention to maintaining it. In the branding process, some brands become inextricably linked to their creators. Think Steve Jobs and Apple, Jeff Bezos and Amazon, Richard Branson and Virgin, and Mark Zuckerberg and Facebook.

Many small businesses have a particularly difficult time with branding because the company's image is so intertwined with its founder and leader. This results from the way in which small businesses are marketed. As small business owners, we rely on networking to build relationships (something that large corporations do not focus on). Those relationships often view us, the owner, as the brand rather than the company itself. Customers want to do business with owners. Customers remember their experiences with owners; the owners' companies are essentially irrelevant. What this means is that the company's brand can get lost in the shuffle, and it can have dire results for owners in the long run. That's what happened to Karen Kerrigan and her not-for-profit organization.

Karen Kerrigan, a political science major from New York, made the connection to DC when she had an internship during college. She was hooked! After several years of working as a fundraiser for various nonprofit organizations, she founded a Washington-based advocacy group, the Small Business Survive Committee, back in the 90s during the Clinton health care debate. Eventually, she changed the name to the Small Business & Entrepreneurship Council (SBE Council), to better reflect the organization's mission and membership. The SBE Council is an advocacy, research, and education group that works to protect the interest of small business and promote entrepreneurship.

From 1994 on, Karen worked tirelessly to establish credibility for the organization so it would be taken seriously by politicians in Washington. She gave a voice to the concerns of small business nationwide for the issues of the day: including health care reform, taxation, and regulation. But in the new millennium, she was ready to move on to other activities. While retaining a connection with the organization, she wanted to transfer the chores of day-to-day leadership to someone else so she could pursue other opportunities.

In 2001, the SBE Council hired someone to run it in Karen's place. She and others interviewed a number of candidates for the job. They selected a person with strong skills in finance, marketing, and operations. Within a year, however, it became clear that things weren't working out. Again, she and others did a thorough job search and found someone with strong people skills and other attributes. After a few months, it again became clear that this was not the right person either.

It took some time for Karen to recognize the problem. It wasn't the people they put in the role of running the SBE Council. The problem was with the public's perception of the SBE Council itself. To many people in Washington, as well as corporate partners and members across the country, Karen *was* the SBE Council. Its brand was her persona. Without Karen, the SBE Council just wasn't the same; it didn't get the same reception among politicos, it couldn't raise as much in contributions as before, and it wouldn't survive without her unless things changed.

After the realization of the problem, Karen and her crew set about to make a change. It became their mission to create strong brand recognition for the SBE Council, independent of Karen, which is something they continue to do today. Toward this end, the SBE Council promotes their annual Indexes: the Small Business Survival Index, the Business Tax Index, and the U.S. Business Policy Index. It also sponsors educational programs, such as its monthly *Growth Without Barriers* webinar series, which helps entrepreneurs with various challenges such as financing, revenue and sales development, marketing, and going global. In addition, the group's small business members are "the face" of the SBE Council. At every opportunity, their entrepreneur supporters appear on television, testify before Congress, and voice the positions of the SBE Council. Karen can still be found on Capitol Hill and promotes the group through her numerous media appearances, but it is the SBE Council's voice that is heard. The organization has yet to transfer control to someone else, but it's well on the way toward this goal.

Looking back from a business perspective, the attempted transfers of governance to someone else were very frustrating for Karen. Despite hiring qualified people, the organization floundered. Even though she worked to transfer leadership, she remained tethered to the organization in the public's perception.

Personally, the inability to transfer management and leadership to someone else was frustrating. She couldn't begin to fully pursue other opportunities, which included international activities related to entrepreneurship. She was keen to move on, yet she wouldn't abandon her baby, the SBE Council, unless she was confident it would thrive in her absence.

Fortunately, over the decade since transfer of management was first attempted, the SBE Council's brand has strengthened. Karen is still part of it, but the SBE Council also has the desired independence in the branding she worked to create and will eventually find a new leader.

Today, while remaining the CEO of the SBE Council, Karen chairs the Center for International Private Enterprise (CIPE), an organization that works to strengthen democracy around the globe through private enterprise and market-oriented reform. She globetrots to spread the message and engage entrepreneurs around the world.

Karen's Lessons

- *Know your brand and cultivate it.* Make sure that all messaging supports the brand you want the public to recognize. It's fine that there is a single well-recognized spokesperson (Karen for the SBE Council and a small business owner for his or her company), but don't confuse the message.

- *Don't rush to transfer power to another leader.* Skills of a job applicant for a leadership position may look good on paper, but you need to find that intangible in the person, which is something that can't be written down. In this case, it was someone who could deliver the SBE Council message and further its brand.

Karen's story is no different from mine with respect to branding. I started my corporation, Big Ideas for Small Business, Inc. in 2000, and today it publishes a newsletter with its name, *Big Ideas for Small Business* and hosts the website BigIdeasForSmallBusiness.com. It's a good business for me; but if I were to try to sell it today, its value would be largely based on my presence in the company. Without me, the brand, Big Ideas for Small Business, would be virtually worthless.

Of course, there are examples of the owner's personality being the brand. Think Oprah, Rachael Ray, and Dr. Phil. But few individuals have the ability to create empires based on their name alone. Most companies should be creating a brand based on their offerings. What products are they selling? What services do they perform? These should shine brighter than the owner's personality.

The problem of the interchangeable brand— company and owner—seems to be commonplace among small businesses. A person starts a business and is not only the technician performing the key activities of the business, but virtually everything else. As the business grows, the solution for many in this position is to work longer hours. The owner doesn't relinquish control over anything, which means that nothing can run without him or her.

Unfortunately, when the business is very dependent on the owner, its valuation suffers. Valuation, for the most part, determines the sale price; and valuation is based on company assets such as equipment, machinery, and intellectual property. It also includes an allowance for goodwill, which, in essence, reflects the brand. When that brand is the owner and will not be part of the business after the sale, the value of goodwill diminishes considerably.

For me, as I'm approaching the last phase of my career, this problem is acute. While I don't have a retirement date in mind and do plan to continue working indefinitely, the business that I've worked so hard to build up would be practically worthless when I die. What can I do about this? Writing this chapter has renewed my resolve to increase brand awareness for my company and create value in the business that someone would pay handsomely for. To build the company's brand, it's necessary to both reposition the messaging and to create a corporate infrastructure that can outlast me. Delegating responsibility for business activities grows the independence of the company. Maybe Apple isn't as great as it was with Steve Jobs, but the business went on successfully to become the first company with a trillion dollar value. With a little focus and change, mine can too.

Barbara's Lessons

- *Think exit strategy.* What would a potential buyer of the business want from the company's brand? It certainly would be something independent of the owner who is selling. Work toward building the company brand and an infrastructure to support the continuation of the company after the owner departs.

- *Leave ego at the door.* One of the reasons why many owners enjoy their personal brand identity is ego. Being recognized is fine. But from a financial perspective, it is meaningless in the long run. Prioritize the goals of the company, which should include building its brand.

Karen Kerrigan

Founder and CEO of the Small Business & Entrepreneurship Council, a 501c(4) nonprofit, nonpartisan advocacy, research, and education organization, Karen is a strong voice on small business issues. She's considered to be one of the leading experts on policies and initiatives  that benefit entrepreneurs. She has received numerous awards and wide recognition, including being named by Forbes Small Business as an advocate in Washington on the Power 30 list. https://www.sbecouncil.org.

Lesson

Don't Mistake Expectations for Reality

Melinda Emerson

SmallBizLady

> *"Oft expectation fails, and most oft there where most it promises; and oft it hits where hope is coldest; and despair most fits."*
>
> —William Shakespeare

am Walton said, "High expectations are the key to everything." As entrepreneurs, we have high expectations that what we set out to do will work. Unfortunately, it doesn't always happen that way. Doing everything in our power sometimes isn't good enough to realize our expectations.

Because of strong expectations, we may ignore the old adage about putting everything in one basket. We believe so strongly in ourselves and assume our expectations will be achieved that, to use some clichés, we burn our bridges and throw caution to the wind. We rely on our expectations coming true rather than dealing with reality as it happens. We follow Andrew Carnegie's advice: "Put all your eggs in one basket and then watch that basket." But watching the basket doesn't always mean that the eggs will hatch and we'll all become Andrew Carnegies. Take the case of Melinda Emerson.

Having started her career as a television producer, she founded and ran a highly successful video company in 1999 called Quintessence Multimedia in Philadelphia, PA. The full-service media production company created public service announcements and did other media work for companies such as Johnson & Johnson, Verizon, Enterprise Rent-A-Car, Novartis, IKEA, Comcast, Radio-One, and the Robert Wood Johnson Foundation. Despite her company's success, Melinda wasn't happy with her work. In 2005 when she was forced to stay in bed for six months because of a risky pregnancy, she had time to think about what she really wanted. And think she did. She emerged from her confinement with a healthy baby boy and an idea about what she wanted to do professionally for the rest of her life. She set a goal for herself—to become America's #1 small business expert.

In furtherance of this goal, Melinda worked on becoming a great national speaker on the subject of small business. She engaged a speaking coach to help her hone her speaking skills. She got involved with the National Speakers Association to learn about securing engagements and becoming a sought-after speaker. And, to add to her "creds," she wrote a book. She had a deadline for her manuscript of September 1, 2008, and worked diligently to meet this deadline, giving up attendance at family barbeques and leisurely vacations. The date of publication for *How to Become Your Own Boss in 12 Months* was set for April 2009, and she was poised to launch the new business of Melinda Emerson, national small business expert. PBS was very interested in featuring Melinda and her book in a pledge drive special (similar to what the network had done with such folks as Suze Orman and Jonathan Pond). The prospects for speaking engagements were heating up. She wound down her video company by not pursuing any new business. She was gearing up personally and professionally to realize her goal of recognition as a small business expert.

But her publisher, Adams Media, had another idea. Because of the state of the economy that resulted from the financial crisis, it wanted to postpone publication until March 2010. Nothing she could do or say would move the publisher to rethink this decision. The publisher was effectively telling her to put her dream and her life on hold for 18 months from the time she handed in the manuscript, which was 11 months more than she had expected. She had gambled her dream on the publication of her book by a set date while letting her former livelihood decay, and she lost.

Personally, this was heartbreaking to say the least. She had busted her tail to finish the book on time. Melinda had been so excited to think that her dream was within her grasp. Visions of fame and fortune faded before her eyes. Family and friends didn't help the situation by saying she should have self-published rather than relying on a publisher.

From a business perspective, the delay was more devastating than could be imagined. She had expected the book to bring her financially rewarding speaking engagements that would replace the income she had been receiving from the video business, which she let fall into decline because she did not think she would be continuing it. She had to regroup—and quickly—to retain her existing clients so she could make a living through this forced hiatus in order to support herself and her family.

When she turned in the manuscript and learned about the publication postponement, a friend suggested that she engage a publicist to help promote the book. The publicist, Cathy Larkin of WebsavvyPR.com, devised a radical plan for

Melinda. Even though the book was not going to be available for sale for a year and a half, Cathy began to promote the book immediately. Her idea was to create interest and demand now so that when the book became available, it would fly off the shelves.

The first thing Cathy wanted Melinda to do was become a force on Twitter, a social media tool that Melinda had not even heard about (Remember, this was 2008.). She immediately went to secure her Twitter name—Melinda Emerson—only to find out that it was already taken! This was another setback, but one that turned out to be a blessing in disguise. Because her name was taken, she had to create one for Twitter; she chose SmallBizLady. The name not only became her Twitter identity; it also became her brand. She used it to make herself known through Twitter and other social media venues so that when the book was ultimately published in March 2010, it sold as she (and her publicist) had wanted. It became a bestseller in no time.

Looking back, if her expectations for overnight success following her completion of the manuscript had not been dashed by an arbitrary decision over which she had no control, who knows what success Melinda might have achieved at that time. It likely would have been less than she ultimately garnered. The setback, in effect, forced her to re-examine her brand and create a much stronger one with the SmallBizLady handle. But certainly, she could have handled things more carefully throughout the process, keeping her business running until her new expert status was well-established. She could have retained high expectations without losing sight of reality.

Melinda's Lessons

- *Don't jettison customers and clients prematurely.* Even if you don't expect to need the revenue in the future, you just never know. Work with existing customers and clients until you can be sure that new revenue streams are actually in place.

- *Hire the best experts.* For personal development or business development, be a lifelong learner. She used speaking coaches and a publicity agent to help her mold the new Melinda.

- *Promote yourself.* Whether or not you write a book that's published, you have to let the public know who you are and what you do. Melinda created an unparalleled persona as *SmallBizLady*. She also launched #SmallBizChat on Twitter and her award-winning blog, https://www.succeedasyourownboss.com.

I too know all about publishers, having worked with a number of different ones over the years. When I had an idea to write my first book, I began to talk with editors at Simon & Schuster. This was back in the 1980s when self-publishing wasn't really an option. I knew people at Simon & Schuster, and they were very encouraging. We talked about the book's concept; I gave them an outline of the chapters; and a contract was promised. So I began to write while waiting for the contract. But every phone call to the editor regarding the contract seemed to be put off; something always came up. By the time I had completed about three quarters of the book, my editor was laid off and I had no contract! Fortunately, he was a good guy and recommended a well-respected book agent who convinced John Wiley & Sons, Inc. to publish *Your Parent's Financial Security.* This book helped to launch my writing career.

Of course, I am no longer taken in by mere flattery and now wait for concrete support for a book project before I begin to put in any serious time and effort. Also, I've learned by observation of many small business owner-writers I know that becoming a published author is not an automatic launch to stardom. For most, it is a painstaking, time-consuming activity that does not translate into any monetary or business reward. However, writing a book can be useful for some entrepreneurs' business goals and, for others, may fulfill a lifelong dream of being an author. Whether to use an established publisher or self publish is a chapter in itself!

Barbara's Lessons

- *Don't bank on promises; wait for things in writing.*
  As a lawyer and a business person with personal experience, I've learned that words don't mean much unless they're written down. It's easy for people to give assurances verbally, but it's the ink that matters. I never start a book now without a contract in hand.

- *Don't have unrealistic expectations about a book's success.*
  Business owners are writing books in droves with the hope that it will give them credibility to speak as an expert on a particular topic, such as marketing, HR, or technology. For some, a book helps; for others, not so much. And, unless you tap into a cultural zeitgeist like E.L. James *(Fifty Shades of Grey)*, don't expect that a business-related book will make you rich. It can, but the expectation should be tempered with reality. There are more than 11,000 business books published each year. Only a handful of them make it to the top of the bestseller charts. A book can be a calling card for an entrepreneur, but the book itself is not likely to create a livelihood.

Melinda Emerson

Melinda F. Emerson, known as SmallBizLady is America's #1 small business expert. As CEO of Quintessence Multimedia, Melinda educates entrepreneurs and Fortune 500 companies on subjects including small business start-up, business development and social media  marketing to fulfill her mission to end small business failure. She writes a weekly column on social media for *The New York Times*. *Forbes* Magazine named her #1 woman for entrepreneurs to follow on Twitter. She hosts #SmallBizChat Wednesdays on Twitter 8–9pm ET to answer small business questions and publishes a resource blog http://www.succeedasyourownboss.com. Melinda is also the bestselling author of *Become Your Own Boss in 12 months: A Month-by-Month Guide to a Business That Works* and *Fix Your Business: A 90-Day Plan to Get Back Your Life and Remove Chaos from Your Business.* https://www.succeedonyourownboss.com

.

Lesson

Don't Let Yourself Become Blinded by Ego

Norm Brodsky

CEO of CitiStorage

> *"Egotism is usually subversive of sagacity."*
> — Marianne Moore, American poet

Self-confidence is an essential trait for small-business owners. It enables us to plunge into the unknown with the belief that we can succeed. It allows us to take on challenges and face opportunities without hesitation. One study in Sweden (http://ideas.repec.org/p/hhs/iuiwop/0887.html) explored the importance of self-confidence to entrepreneurship and found a direct correlation between self-confidence and business creation. Those with self-confidence tend to start businesses. However, when a business owner becomes overconfident, problems can arise.

Too much of a good thing can mean trouble. Too much self-confidence can lead to an inflated ego, which is really nothing more than an exaggerated sense of selfworth. This trait can then lead to poor business judgment, as an inflated ego can be used to justify actions due to the thinking that "you're always right." You can become blind to the realities of the business and about what's happening in the world outside the business. Ironically, part of the problem with developing an inflated ego is that, by definition, you can't see it happening. At least that's what happened to Norm Brodsky a number of years ago.

Norm Brodsky went to law school to please his mother, but he knew after a short stint in practice that being a lawyer wasn't for him. Business was his true calling. He started one company, then another, becoming a serial entrepreneur— something he remains to this day. In the early 1980s, he started a specialized delivery company that provided overnight and long-distance deliveries of documents. The company expanded over a period of eight years, eventually operating in 18 states. A major part of his customer base was financial institutions that received overnight deliveries of printed financial materials. In those eight years, he grew the business from zero to $140 million in annual revenue. Then, on Monday, October 19, 1987, "Black Monday," the stock market crashed. The Dow Jones Industrial Average dropped from 2,247 to 1,739 by the close of Black Monday (And it took two years for the market to get back to pre-crash levels.). To put things in perspective, the current Dow of around 26,000 (as of August 2018) would have to lose nearly 6,000 points in a single day to equal the drop of Black Monday. Suddenly, a good chunk of Norm's customers in the financial industry no longer needed his services.

As if that weren't enough, a new technological device called the facsimile (fax) machine became omnipresent at the same time. The patent for the first fax machine was issued to a Scottish inventor in 1843, but it wasn't until the mid-1980s that fax machines became small enough and inexpensive enough for businesses to adopt their use. By the time of the crash in 1987, most businesses owned a fax machine. I bought my first fax machine in 1986 and felt so technology empowered! Remember thermal paper? Faxing meant there was a dramatically reduced need for overnight deliveries of documents. Sure, there continued to be some need by law firms and other businesses for document delivery services where only originals were acceptable, but the size of the market had been permanently shrunk.

Norm never saw this two-pronged attack coming—neither the fax machine nor the crash. No one ever really knows which technological device will be a winner— remember eight-track tapes? The adoption of the fax machine was nearly as rapid as the adoption of the iPad and mobile credit card readers for use in business today. And who could have predicted the crash? Only a select few Wall Street experts expressed predictions about a crash, and they were scoffed at.

Even though Norm was blindsided, the truth is that neither the stock market crash nor the new technology was really his undoing. It was his self-confidence or inflated ego (whichever you want to call it) that got him into trouble. His company went from $140 million in sales annually to zero in just eight months. Why? The primary reason for the rapid downward spiral was that he had pledged the assets of one company to create another company based on the belief that he couldn't fail. This financing arrangement of making companies interdependent on each other was not solid enough to get by. When one company faltered, the other was not in a strong enough financial position to support the debt service that the leveraged financing arrangement entailed.

The overnight document express business essentially collapsed overnight (pun intended), but he is still convinced that he could have survived if he had not been so highly leveraged. The leveraging meant that the business could not withstand the adverse changes created by outside forces (the crash and the fax).

The end of the business forced Norm to lay off thousands of workers across the country. This was a devastating experience for him. It was the first time he really appreciated that he was responsible for more than just himself and his family. He had thousands of individuals and their families depending on him for a paycheck, and he let them down. If you've ever had to lay off even a single worker, you can imagine the personal angst that Norm experienced from his mega-layoff.

His immediate response to the demise of this business could have been to blame outside forces—the stock market crash killing his customer base and the new technology essentially replacing some of the service that his company had provided. But Norm didn't put the blame on these outside forces. Instead, he became introspective about the experience. Why did he *really* fail? The bottom line for his failure turned out to lie within himself. It was his ego; he thought he was invincible in business and couldn't fail. He believed that leveraging was the smart way to expand his empire and that there was no risk to this position. He failed to heed the advice of Colin Powell, who said, "Avoid having your ego so close to your position that when your position falls, your ego goes with it."

Fortunately, the failure didn't dampen Norm's enthusiasm for creating businesses. Today Norm continues to run his existing businesses and continually looks for new business opportunities; however, he no longer leverages his current businesses to launch new ventures.

Looking back now, he can't understand why he took the financial position that he did. It was like building a house of cards, which needs only one to fall in order to bring the entire house down. He did, however, learn some important lessons from this failure.

Norm's Lessons

- *Check your ego at the door.* Remain self-confident, but don't get cocky. It can cloud your vision and seduce you into making horrendous errors in your business.

- *Don't leverage one business with another.* Obviously, he learned that leveraging one business with another is not the way to go. This rather-apparent lesson may not be so clear to others. He had to experience the failure himself to learn the lesson.

- *A business failure is always the fault of the owner.* Outside forces can trigger a collapse, but it is up to the entrepreneur to foresee, plan, and ultimately accept responsibility for a company's demise.

- *Start a business with a number in mind that you're willing to lose.* In the 1990s, Norm obtained a license from the New York City Fire Department to display FDNY on gift items. He projected that it would cost $1 million to launch the gift business in New York City. As has become his practice, he built in another 25% ($250,000) to the total amount he was ultimately willing to risk on this particular venture. Then 9/11 happened; and for those who were not in the metropolitan area following this catastrophic event, the business climate was bleak. He had already invested $1.25 million without making a go of the business, so he folded it. He had reached the dollar limit he set in advance for the amount of risk he was willing to take.

I wish I had known Norm years ago when I started my newsletter, *Big Ideas for Small Business*®. I could have saved thousands of dollars. I launched it in July 2002 as a print publication with a subscription price of $29.95. I thought that the price was right and the market ripe for the taking. I was brimming with self-confidence. There were no other newsletters specifically for small businesses available at the time, and my sample issue drew favorable feedback from many respected business luminaries. Sure, there were some magazines that gave me competition such as *Entrepreneur*, but I thought the quality of my content and the absence of advertising would be a draw. Over the next four years, I continued to try to grow subscriptions. I ran various promotions; I made good connections; and I tried very hard and continued to be overly self-confident. What I failed to appreciate because of my extreme self-confidence was the growing trend of getting information from the Internet.

Each month, I incurred printing, labeling, and mailing costs that well exceeded my subscription revenues, not to mention my time in dealing with these tasks. I continued to let the print newsletter be a cash (and time) drain on my business for four long years! In year five, I took the newsletter to the web but continued to charge for readership. Again, I failed to see the ancillary impact of the Internet—people expected their information to be free! After a year of trying to sell subscriptions to my e-newsletter, I changed my business model, repositioning the newsletter from a product to a promotion. I now give away the content to enhance my role as an expert and monetize this through content deals with Fortune 500 companies.

Looking back, I should have done a few things better: Like Norm, I should have kept my overconfidence in check; I should have set a limit on how much I was willing to lose before folding or changing course; and I should have better understood the impact of new technology.

Barbara's Lessons

- *Hoping for improvement in sales is not part of the business plan.* Create a marketing plan and, after implementing it, reassess the situation. Maybe outside forces, such as a technology change, warrant a revision in the marketing plan. If you fall short of your goals, take responsibility and also take action. Make decisions that can advance your business rather than simply repeating the same efforts. Work smarter, not harder.

- *Limit financial exposure.* Even if you have the money to continue to support a losing company (or marketing a losing product or service), don't do so indefinitely. At the start, set a dollar limit on how much you're willing to invest in trying to make a go of things. Once you reach the limit and still have no success, admit defeat so you can move on to a potentially better opportunity.

Resources

A certain amount of self-confidence can be a great thing, but do what you can to benefit from the input of others. Consider joining an executive and peer advisory group designed to critique your situation and ideas. This requires a commitment of time and money, but it may be well worth the cost. Check for eligibility requirements, which may depend on company revenue or other factors; some groups are by invitation only. Examples of advisory groups:

Chief Executive Officers Club, Inc.

https://www.ceoclubs.org

CEO Roundtable

https://www.ceo-roundtable.com

Entrepreneurs' Organization

https://www.eonetwork.org

TEC Canada

https://www.tec-canada.com

Vistage

https://www.vistage.com

Women's Presidents Organization

https://www.womenpresidentsorg.com

You can also work with SCORE (https://www.score.org) or a Small Business Development Center (SBDC) (https://www.sba. gov/content/small-business-development-centers-sbdcs) for free. Here you can get feedback from someone with former business experience. (This is not a peer advisory group.)

Norm Brodsky

Norm is the founder of CitiStorage, a records management company founded in 1990 to serve the New York metropolitan area, as well as seven previous start-ups. He is a three-time winner in the Inc. *500* annual listing. He began writing a monthly column entitled *Street Smarts* for *Inc.* magazine with Bo Burlingham in 1995, which led to their book *The Knack*.

Lesson

Be Careful Who You Trust

Peter Justen

Chairman at The Enrepreneurial Ecosystem

> *"The only true wisdom is in knowing you know nothing."*
>
> —Socrates

As entrepreneurs, we tend to be risk takers, and we'll boldly go where others fear to tread. Being a risk taker is a double-edged sword. On one hand, it means we'll try things even if there is no assurance of success. We "poohpooh" the naysayers because we believe in ourselves and think we have a chance to succeed. For the most part, being a risk-taker can be a good thing. It is this attitude that enables entrepreneurs to forsake a paycheck from an employer and not play it safe in order to start their own ventures in uncharted waters.

On the other hand, we risk takers can overlook or minimize problems and fail to employ the caution that's advisable to avoid disaster. We leap before we look; we make favorable assumptions; we think we know it all. And that can prove to be a bad thing—especially when it comes to taking a risk on people, both those we hire and those we partner with. We want to believe that everyone is honorable, reliable, and enterprising like we are, but that isn't always the case. Even an experienced and successful business owner can succumb to making bad choices in people.

Peter Justen was a successful entrepreneur in the Washington, D.C. area who had started and exited a number of profitable ventures. One such venture was MyBizHomepage, which he launched in 2006 to help small businesses stay on top of their business finances and avoid money woes. It became a highly successful, unique dashboard display product for small business owners in the

U.S. and more than 45 other countries. I loved it! By logging on, just like looking at the dashboard of my car, I could see all of my vital financial information in one glance. It would search through my QuickBooks data and tell me when I was expecting payments as well as when I had to make payments. I could use it to easily monitor cash flow at a glance, and the best part was that this online resource was free! In just three years, there were thousands of users. Pete, who is passionate about entrepreneurship and small business and the effect they have on the economy, was busy trekking around the country, demonstrating how his site was a no-brainer aid to small businesses. "We felt that we had an awfully good chance of becoming the world standard for real-time, high-integrity data on small-to-emerging growth companies, something the industry sorely needs."

In other words, Pete was on a roll; his site was named by *Inc.* as one of the 10 must-haves of 2008, and he was confident that the company would continue on its growth path.

Much of the early success of his company was due to its unique product and positioning in the market, but Pete knew he had to move fast to keep up with the growth. "I knew in order to continue to grow at the pace we were, I needed to add people I knew whose abilities I trusted. Our existing tech team was good, but we had to push it to the next level." Pete had one person in mind (I'll call him Harry.). Pete had known Harry for 15 years, and he had no reason to *not* feel confident about Harry's abilities and loyalty. Pete had worked with Harry years earlier and helped Harry build his career. Pete hired him to head up his IT department and had Harry relocate to Virginia to become the Chief Technology Officer of MyBizHomepage.com. As a trusted friend and someone new to town, Harry dined at Pete's home two or three nights every month. He was friendly with Pete's children. Harry was a skilled techie who helped develop the computer code needed for the company to meet its ever-growing subscriber base as well as offer new options and features to stay in the forefront of the market.

In the fourth quarter of 2008, Pete learned that his "friend" Harry and two other company executives were planning to launch their own company using Pete's intellectual property (IP). They were all terminated immediately, but that didn't stop the problem; it was just getting started—and in full force. In order to grab Pete's IP legally and without paying for it, they had to drive Pete out of business. Harry set a plot to do just that. He launched a series of attacks against Pete's site using "logic bombs," which are code that he had inserted surreptitiously into Pete's program. They were designed to blow up under certain circumstances, such as a lapse of time or a specific command. When the bombs "exploded," they disrupted or deleted data, including backup data. Pete tried to have new IT people work on the problem, but the bombs had been planted so cleverly and carefully that when corrections were made from one explosion, another bomb blew up, ultimately causing the loss of all of the code for

MyBiz Homepage.com as well as all of the data from the company's customer base. Pete reflected that trying to fix the data problem was like playing whack-a-mole at the carnival— smashing down one only caused another to arise.

Harry's devastating attack didn't stop with the theft of the code and the destruction of data. Despite the cyber attacks and loss of investment capital, Pete, with the help of outside IT people, kept limping along. Because the efforts to destroy Pete's company were unsuccessful, Harry then made things personal. He continued his cyber attack with a series of vicious defamatory attacks against Pete, his parents, some of Pete's board members, and even his five sons and daughter. Their Facebook, LinkedIn, and Outlook accounts were hacked; and emails were sent to their contact lists with outrageous accusations against Pete and his family of fraud, theft, pending indictments, misuse of corporate funds, and other defamatory and untrue statements. He even made physical threats against Pete's children. And he created websites on which to display fake information about Pete and his family, saying Pete was a felon on the run from the law and that Pete's father (who had been deceased for 16 years) and his 89-year-old mother were co-conspirators about to be indicted. These attacks were expanded to mobile devices as well. Harry made multiple demands for money— $10,000 to $50,000—to stop his cyber attacks. Imagine the emotional toll that hearing the threats and defamatory statements took on Pete and his family!

There is no doubt that trusting the wrong guy represented a major failure for Pete, but this didn't stop him from moving ahead. It was time for Pete to fight back. He went to the authorities and learned that his "friend" of 15 years lived off the grid with no address, driver's license, credit cards, tax returns, or any other items that would have created a paper trail; he also had convictions of theft in two states. Pete, who describes himself like a puppy that's got hold of an old sock, did not give in to blackmail and was prepared to see that Harry was stopped. He worked with authorities to find Harry with the hope that his tormentor would eventually be prosecuted for cyber crimes, blackmail, and other criminal activities (no indictments yet).

C.S. Lewis said that "When things go wrong, they usually go on getting worse for some time," and that's what happened to Pete. His debacle came at the height of the global economic recession, making it virtually impossible to raise funds to recreate the old company or start a new one. Pete refused to become a victim and take the safe road—settling for a job or perhaps even retirement. Instead, his entrepreneurial spirit refused to be defeated. Eventually, Pete found the necessary capital and was able to launch a new business: FivePlus (www.fiveplus.co), a new and improved business monitoring tool that helps small business owners keep track of finances and their networks. The new products incorporated social media, mobile media, and other new technology. Features of the new FivePlus dashboard included:

- Automatic retrieval of data from QuickBooks
- Data that is converted to readable, understandable, and actionable information
- Data that is displayed in real time on your desktop
- Alerts so you can act before trouble hits
- Platforms to expand your business network
- More features including a mobile offering that works across all platforms, and Outlook integration, along with a "freemium model" where basic services are offered at no charge

Ultimately, Pete's failure to discover early on who Harry really was resulted in a complete loss of two years of development and about $3.5 million in investments. But Pete is certainly wiser for his experience. He learned that he had to retain control of his company's code and could not give anyone unfettered access to the company's core asset. He also learned that people are not always what they seem to be, and that it's necessary to check out claims made by potential employees or partners. These lessons have been put to good use in his new company.

Looking back on those days, there were things Pete should have known—behavior patterns that didn't fit a loyal person that he should have reacted to. He kept brushing them off because he trusted Harry. "The quandary is . . . I've always thought you gain loyalty by being loyal. While I still believe that is true, I now understand that you have to start with a trustworthy person to begin with."

Pete's Lessons

- *Determine at the start whether someone is not only capable, but also trustworthy.* Don't just go with your gut feelings on this. "Trust but verify," said President Ronald Reagan in regard to his dealings with the Soviet Union. It's fine to see the best in people and believe that they are who they say they are. But it's easy . . . and wise . . . to check things out. Check out the people you plan to partner with. Also do background checks on any job applicants you want to hire (See resources at the end of this chapter.). Background checks are easy to do today, and they don't cost a lot. Condition their employment upon a satisfactory background check.

- *Act decisively when you detect a problem.* Don't just hope things will get better. This may entail turning to law enforcement agencies or an attorney who can represent your interests.

- *Fight back.* Defamatory statements (that are false) posted by bullies or disgruntled former employees can be offset by publicizing your side of the story.

- *Recognize that cyber attacks can come from internal sources.* Protections such as malware, firewalls, and anti-virus software won't protect you from internal attacks; your vigilance will. Keep a copy of critical code and infrastructure in a secure environment.

- *Don't be discouraged from being in business merely because you experience a failure, no matter how devastating.* Pete was able to start a new and better business to continue serving the small business community.

- *Take heart in learning who your true friends really are.* Whenever you go through a catastrophic event, such as the cyber attacks Pete experienced, you quickly see who continues to stand by you and who does not.

Unfortunately, I had a similar experience and hitched my wagon to folks I thought were stars but turned out to be only nice people with little star power. Years before reality shows became popular, I had the idea to launch a show that would help small businesses out of the jams they found themselves in. My vision for the show was to find a business, identify the problem it faced, and then offer no-cost or low-cost fixes. I expected to follow up six months later to see whether the suggested changes had worked to solve the problem.

The team I chose to work with claimed to have "connections" in the television industry and I took them at their word. It turned out that they had known a few people but weren't really as well connected as they appeared to be. I never checked out their claims or pressed them for information that would have led me to make a more informed decision about my business partners. I invested a good deal of money and effort in a project that simply went nowhere. There was no big blowup among the team; the project just fizzled and all I had from the experience was a hard lesson and a big tax write-off!

Barbara's Lessons

- *Leave emotion out of a decision to partner with someone in business.* Like a marriage, a business partnership theoretically lasts until death.

  Unfortunately, like more than half of all marriages today, business partnerships don't always work out when they are founded on misperceptions. You may like your partners personally and think you can work well together, but you need to take a critical look at what each person brings to the team— money, skills, vision, etc.

- *Hold partners to their end of the bargain.* If a partner promises to do something, make sure it gets done. Wishing for the best won't produce results.

Resources

Here are some resources to help you:

BackgroundCheck.org gives you some basics about background checks.

https://www.backgroundcheck.org

BackgroundChecks.com provides businesses with background check solutions, from employment and education verification to licensing and more. It also offers employee background monitoring.

https://www.backgroundchecks.com

Sterling Talen Solutions provides employment screening services.

https://www.employeescreen.com

Peter Justen

Peter is the Chairman at the Entrepreneurial Econsystem which helps emerging growth economies create and stabilize small businesses. Previously, he founded MyBizHomepage.com, PowerWorx, and Five Plus. He currently serves as the chair of the advisory board for the Henry F. Byrd Jr. School of Business at Shenandoah University, and previously he was the chairman of the Washington Symphony. Peter has been profiled in Business Week, Inc.com, Fox News, *The Wall Street Journal*, CNN Money, and Forbes.com.

Lesson

Document All Business Practices . . . and Prepare for All Contingencies

Susan Solovic

Co-founder and CEO of SBTV

> *"God is love, but get it in writing."*
>
> —Gypsy Rose Lee

When I was transitioning from my law practice to my information services business, one of the first business books I read was Michael E. Gerber's *The E Myth Revisited: Why Most Small Businesses Don't Work and What to Do About It*. It completely changed my thinking about how to operate a business. He explained the importance of a business being able to replicate what it did in order to be in a position to grow: "The Entrepreneurial Model has less to do with what's done in a business and more to do with how it's done. The commodity isn't what's important—the way it's delivered is."

Most small businesses are so enamored by their offering (the product or service they feature) that they often operate like a hobbyist—doing what they do because they love it, but failing to do what's needed to make it a business that can grow. Unlike franchises, they don't systemize their operations. If the owner isn't around, the business will likely flounder because no one else knows what to do. No matter how great the business idea may be, it's vital for the company to recognize the importance of creating systems and writing them down. Without them, the business can easily fail when the unexpected occurs. That's what Susan Solovic found out the hard way.

Susan, an attorney by trade, co-founded SBTV (Small Business TV) in 2003 with two men she knew in St. Louis, Missouri. SBTV quickly became a unique online television forum for small businesses (It was like YouTube for small business before YouTube existed.). The stature of the business was unparalleled. In fact, the IRS even ran informational material on SBTV. And Susan, as a former beauty queen and articulate small-business expert, shared her knowledge with viewers on a regular basis on SBTV. By mid-2006, SBTV was voted as the best investment opportunity of the year, presenting to a Venture Forum event in Silicon Valley (The Venture Forum was called Women's Technology Cluster then, and is known today as ASTIA) and it also received a Stevie Award for the most innovative company with under 100 employees. But the year wasn't over yet.

In October of that year, Susan was attending a Make Mine a Million event in New York City for women entrepreneurs seeking to get their companies to over $1 million in revenue. While there, she received a phone call from Michael Kelley, the COO of SBTV. "Find a quiet place and sit down," he said. She walked into a broom closet to continue the conversation. He told her that he had just been diagnosed with stage 3 melanoma and was given six months to live. Literally, in a flash, Susan's world passed before her eyes.

Personally, the news was devastating to say the least. Michael was not only her business partner, but he was also someone she cared about—someone who had a 12-year-old daughter.

From a business perspective, the news was just as gut-wrenching. Michael had created a proprietary delivery platform for SBTV, and the company had just started the process of getting a patent for it. Unfortunately, everything about the platform—the password, how it worked, and how to maintain it—was in Michael's head. Nothing was on paper. He immediately began undergoing surgeries and treatments that left him in no shape to share the highly technical and complex secrets of the platform with Susan or anyone else. Unless the platform's secrets could be decoded, there would be no SBTV. Without it, the once-promising company, named as the best investment opportunity of the year, would go under.

To put in perspective how devastating the news about Michael was to SBTV, within six months, Susan's other partner developed severe high blood pressure and blew out his retina. Fortunately, he got his blood pressure under control and could continue with SBTV.

Putting emotions aside, Susan had to address the critical problem for her company: how to immediately get on top of the platform on which SBTV ran. She hired a friend of Michael's whom he recommended to work through the platform's code, but his work alone was not enough. She also had to engage outside consultants to deal with the problem. The solution wasn't cheap, but luckily SBTV was profitable in 2006, the year of the calamity. While SBTV posted a loss in 2007, the year in which the problem was being addressed, it was able to return to profitability by 2008. It took several years to really iron out all of the problems, including a change in management, and put the company on the right track.

While Susan is no longer involved with SBTV, the company continues to support an advertising and content network of 285 websites. Michael fought a good fight and lived longer than his doctors had expected; sadly he died in 2010 after waging a valiant battle against his cancer.

From living through this horrific experience, Susan learned that every business, no matter how small, needs what she calls "bus books." These are procedures and business information that's written down for others to use in case someone gets hit by a bus. Hopefully there won't be any bus accident; but if the worst happens, there will at least be the necessary guidance in place for the business to go on.

Susan's Lessons

- *Document business processes.* Every business should document each job description, code, and all other business aspects so that the business can function if someone is not there. This also enables the business to be replicated, an asset if the business wants to expand. For example, a restaurant that has done business process documentation can easily open a second location that provides the same dining experience as the original location.

- *Be mentally prepared for the unexpected.* No one can ever plan for illness or accidents, but they happen nonetheless. Despite emotions for the partner, employee, or investor experiencing the problem, you as the business owner must steel yourself to go forward. Other people are depending on you to set the example and address the needs at hand.

Like Susan, I had my own "bus book" experience. When I started my newsletter as a subscription-based print edition, I tried to sell the concept to a number of large corporations. I met with the head of the small business division of Chase Bank in the Wall Street area of New York City and had a great chat. The one problem that he had with adopting my newsletter for his small business customers was that I was a one-person shop. How would the newsletter be produced on time if something happened to me? It never occurred to me that this would be a problem.

Like other small-business owners, if we make commitments, we must get things done. In my 35 years in business, despite giving birth and raising children, going through a messy divorce, experiencing various medical ailments (including severing a tendon on my index finger), and having power outages that prevented access to my computer, I never missed a deadline. I found a way to get things done because they *had* to get done.

However, in order to move forward with Chase, I had to arrange for a backup editor/writer for my newsletter. I signed an agreement with another newsletter writer I knew that could complete an issue if I couldn't. We agreed on a fee that would be paid for each issue he completed and discussed my vision for the newsletter. As it turns out, in all these years since signing that agreement, I've never needed to rely on his services.

Looking back, however, I can see now that having a fallback position is not a bad idea for me or any other small business. Making arrangements to have someone else do your work is sound business practice. After all, don't psychiatrists refer patients to other psychiatrists during their vacations? In order to have the backup when needed, it's not only necessary to find the right person, but also to put in writing what has to be done. The backup psychiatrist should be given access to patient files. In my case, providing a template for my newsletter, as well as putting my backup on my mailing list to receive all newsletter issues so that he knew what topics had already been covered, were the best ways to lay out the scope of the work.

Barbara's Lessons

- *Acknowledge that disruptive things can happen.* Despite the trait of self-reliance and a can-do attitude, something unexpected can occur. An illness, accident, or other unforeseen event can put you, or some key employee, out of commission— temporarily or permanently.

- *Get backup for key tasks.* Designate a person who can fill your shoes when necessary. Give this person the tools to do your job, including access to passwords, files, and other information that's key to your work.

Susan Solovic

Susan Solovic is CEO of Susan Solovic Media and the former co-founder and CEO of SBTV. She is an expert personality on ABC News, Fox Business Network, MSNBC, CNN, and a host of other media. A sought-after keynote speaker, Susan is an award-winning entrepreneur and adjunct professor of entrepreneurship at Saint Louis University where she also serves on the advisory board for the John Cook School of Business Entrepreneurial Studies at Saint Louis University. She has written several books, including her recent bestseller *The One-Percent Edge: Small Changes that Guarantee Relevance and Build Sustainable Success.* She also provides podcasts, blogs, and other information for small business at ItsYourBiz.com, which is powered by SBTV.

Lesson

Don't Let Desperation
Dictate Action

Tim Berry

Founder and chairman of Palo Alto Software

> *"We all need money, but there are degrees
> of desperation."*
> —Anthony Burgess, English novelist
> and critic

Smart people can make dumb decisions. When a person feels desperate, he can make bad choices that, in better times, he would have never made. Bad decisions that result from really wanting something have nothing to do with education, experience, or even common sense. All you have to do is look at the tabloids to see many powerful men who have let lust steer them off the high road.

It's no different in business. Desperation can drive us in the wrong direction. As a deadline approaches, it's tempting to cut corners and do a less-than-great job. When money is tight, it's too easy to accept an offer of help, no matter how poor the terms of the agreement may be. That's what happened to Tim Berry early in the life of his business.

Tim Berry was an MBA graduate who got his practical business training in Silicon Valley in the 1970s and early 1980s. By 1983, he had an idea for a business and was ready to go out on his own. He started Palo Alto Software, named after the city he lived in, to help the user craft a business plan. The company incorporated in 1988 and at that time had no employees; Tim alone worked on the software product for creating business plans. Since his software wasn't a money maker yet, he supported his family with consulting. In 1992, he and his family moved from Palo Alto, California, to Eugene, Oregon. The move was motivated by personal reasons; he wanted the lifestyle that Oregon could offer his family. He continued to work on his business in the new location.

Finally, Tim had written enough business plans and had developed the software to the point that he could start to sell a Business Plan Toolkit. The product was great, but it was less than a financial success at the beginning. After four years of struggling to market the product, he wasn't even breaking even. He wanted to ditch the consulting (he was working one week a month in Japan) and make Palo Alto his future. In order to do this, he needed someone to help him sell his product.

Tim met Stan (not his real name) at a local Chamber of Commerce event. Stan had a very impressive background. He'd been the president of a software company where he'd taken sales from $500,000 to $2.7 million. Stan was a great talker, and he offered Tim a ray of hope. Tim thought maybe Stan knew what to do to get sales moving. Tim was desperate to sell more product, so Tim made a deal with Stan in 1993.

The deal was based on sales. If Stan could sell $1 million in the first year, $2 million in the second year, and $3 million in the third, Tim would give Stan 50% of the business. Give away half the company? Tim felt he had nothing to lose. If sales didn't pick up appreciably, he'd soon own 100% of nothing.

Stan turned out to be a great salesman. He easily got past gatekeepers to make the sales to distributors. Unfortunately, Tim forgot to consider that sales are not necessarily a good measurement of revenue for a company. Stan was focusing solely on sales that he could book in order to meet the targeted sales figure for obtaining ownership in the business. You see, Stan was doing anything he could to make it happen—like giving two free units with each one he sold or offering huge discounts to book the sales. This turned out to be a financial nightmare for Palo Alto Software.

On top of that, Tim's deal with Stan didn't take into account the true nature of software sales at that time. Tim's first mistake—acting in desperation—was compounded by another mistake—not understanding the concept of sell-through. The company had to agree to buy back unsold items at the same price that they had been bought in the first place. This is called sell-through, a concept that applies when selling through distributors. It means the sale really isn't final until it's in the hands of consumers. As a result, the numbers weren't adding up. The company was accumulating a growing liability for unsold boxes in stores. The company had booked sales of more than a million units, but it was sitting on 300,000 unsold units on store shelves.

To make matters worse, Tim and Stan couldn't agree on how to fix the problem. Stan wanted the company to physically do the packaging and to buy a piece of equipment to help with this. Tim was opposed to it, but he gave in to keep the peace. This obviously didn't fix the problem. In February of 1994, at a national event joining publishers with the big software distributors, Tim and Stan discovered together that the products weren't selling, stores were sending them back unopened, about a quarter of a million dollars booked as sales in 1993 had never really been sold through to consumers, and distributors were going to be sending them back for full refunds. The company was in deep trouble; something had to change quickly if Palo Alto Software was to survive.

Fortunately, both men agreed to seek the help of a local attorney they each respected who could mediate a solution. Stan realized that the company was facing liabilities, and he wanted nothing more to do with the promised ownership that would effectively saddle him with these liabilities. He was willing to walk away from the deal. All he took was assembly equipment (the item he coerced Tim to agree to buying) that he could use in a fulfillment business he wanted to start.

Tim knew it was time to take an honest look at his company and why it was struggling. He realized that one of the reasons his product sat on the shelves was that the packaging was terrible. He had to spiff up the packaging so consumers would at least view the product. Another reason it wasn't selling was that computing had advanced beyond what his product was offering. He had to upgrade the programming or risk becoming noncompetitive.

It was 1994, Tim had three children in college, his consulting in Japan was coming to an end, and his business was still struggling. After his honest look at the company, Tim moved into action. He addressed each of his problems individually to find solutions that worked!

- He turned to a local print shop to upgrade the packaging, adding a picture and quotes on the back of the box.

- He used sales reps to get the product on shelves, paying them a percentage of revenue (taking into account sell-through).

- He used local programmers to add the features he wanted the software to have, such as a control menu.

By January 1995, Palo Alto Software was on its way. The product received excellent reviews and began selling well. He was able to settle all the liabilities incurred during the Stan period. By the end of the year, the company had eight employees and had made $1.8 million.

Looking back, the Stan episode was a painful learning experience. Personally, Tim felt as desperate after parting ways with Stan as he had when he first joined forces with him. He only got through the experience with the support of his wife. From a business perspective, Tim learned some hard lessons. Stan wasn't a bad person, but Tim made a bad deal because of desperation. He learned about the realities of sharing ownership, needing a better understanding of financial details, and finding solutions with local help.

Today, Palo Alto Software is the premium business planning solution, and Tim has retired from the day-to-day operations of the business. Sales figures are private because the company continues to be a closely held family owned business, but Palo Alto Software has become the company that Tim dreamed it would be!

Tim's Lessons

- *Don't give away equity too easily.* You can usually achieve what you want by sharing revenue instead.

- *Only partner with someone who has the same goals as you do.* Talk things through upfront to make sure that there's consensus about the direction and action of the business.

- *Understand the financial ins and outs of your industry.* The concept of sell-through may or may not apply to your business, but there may be unique financial arrangements that you had better know about before you run into problems.

- *Find solutions locally.* There is an array of talent across this country. You don't have to go to big cities or abroad to find the help you need to run your business; check out the resources you have in your own backyard.

Desperation is a feeling I can certainly relate to. In the 1980s, I went through a terrible divorce at a time when I had two very young children and three mortgages (one on my home and two on investment properties owned jointly with my husband). I was receiving no support of any kind from my husband to pay all the bills. I was entirely on my own as a parent and working full-time.

The experience made me feel sick every day. At that time, I experienced the greatest sense of desperation in the mornings. I'd waken early with a sinking feeling in the pit of my stomach. What was I going to do? How would I support my children and see my way through a financial mess? Some days, the only thing I could think about was how to get through the day.

I combated the feeling of desperation by taking action. I pressed my attorney to work out a quick settlement. I didn't ask for any child support or hold out other payments from my ex; I just wanted a clean break and an equal division of the property. The investment properties were put on the market and eventually sold, allowing those mortgages to be paid off.

To help me move ahead, I put my pencil to paper to figure out how much I needed to earn to stay in my home and support my children. I set this financial goal and, by doing so, felt optimistic for the first time in a long time. I realized that my goal was not far-fetched, and it turned out to be doable. I was able to achieve it by ramping up my law practice, expanding my writing, and growing my business. I remained in the same house until I recently relocated, my children are grown, my practice has been closed, but my business is booming and doing better than I could have imagined in those mornings of desperation.

Barbara's Lessons

- *Combat desperation with action.* Determine what's making you feel desperate, then create a plan of action to address the cause of the desperation. If it's money (like Tim), find a way to make more without selling out or making bad decisions.

- *Be optimistic.* It may sound easier to say than do, but thinking positively goes a long way toward achieving goals. Walt Disney said, "If you dream it, you can do it," and I embrace this philosophy.

Tim Berry

Founder and chairman of Palo Alto Software, Tim has been called the "Father of Business Planning." He has an MBA from Stanford and has written a number of books, including *The Plan-as-You-Go Business Plan.* Now that his, daughter Sabrina Parsons is, president of the company, he devotes time to being the official business planning coach at Entrepreneur.org and a member of the Willamette Angel Conference, an angel investment group. https://www.TimBerry.com

Lesson

Look Carefully
Before You Leap

W. Kenneth Yancey, Jr.

CEO of SCORE

> *"Plans are nothing; planning is everything."*
> —Dwight Eisenhower, President

One of the main characteristics of entrepreneurs is enthusiasm. FreshBooks listed enthusiasm as among the top six characteristics that define an entrepreneur. Entrepreneurs universally have a passion for what they do. Unfortunately, it's all too common to see enthusiasm get the better of some business owners. They have a great idea for a company, a product, or a service, and they jump right in. They may create a plan of sorts, such as a launch date for the new venture, and they may incorporate all of the necessary planning components and checkpoints that go a long way to ensuring a successful outcome.

Don't misunderstand me. There's a place for enthusiasm, and it shouldn't be curbed (no offense to Larry David). Without enthusiasm, apathy can kill or delay progress on projects. But enthusiasm should be combined with planning. Planning for any new project or venture entails a number of steps:

- Define the project—its purpose, goals, and objectives.

- Delineate the scope of the project—the time it will take and the funds it will require.

- Set roles and responsibilities—who oversees the project and who else is involved (whether internal or outsourced).

---

[1] www.bookfresh.com/resources/article/what-are-the-characteristics-of-entrepreneurs/

- Define metrics and set milestones to keep track of the progress.

- Create a communications plan—how and when feedback from stakeholders (staff, customers, vendors, investors, community leaders, or others) will be obtained.

While the steps in planning may be easy to outline, they are not as easy to implement. As I said, many business owners, in the throes of excitement, skip these steps entirely and proceed immediately to implementation. Other business owners may not fully understand or excel at these planning essentials and, as a result, have little planning in hand (or incorrect conclusions in place) when implementation begins. Any business owner, even with experience and enthusiasm, can easily fall into the trap of leaping before looking more closely at the project.

That's what happened to Ken Yancey. A banker by trade, he became the executive director of SCORE in 1993 and its CEO in 2000. SCORE, as a resource partner with the U.S. Small Business Administration (SBA), provides free counseling to businesses across the country. SCORE is a nonprofit association that was founded in 1964 and today has more than 13,000 volunteer mentors in 354 offices nationwide. As it says on SCORE's website: "SCORE has served more than 10 million existing and aspiring small-business owners since inception and helps to create more than 58,000 new businesses and over 71,000 new jobs annually." I personally know what a great resource SCORE is for small businesses because I've worked with SCORE on both sides of the desk: as a small-business owner seeking guidance on a business plan I had for a venture launched a number of years ago, and as a speaker to the volunteers in local SCORE offices. Ken has been a big part of the growth and success that SCORE has achieved over the years. But no matter how successful you've been in the past, there's always room for potential failure, as Ken recently found out.

In 2010, Ken and his staff determined that it was time to upgrade SCORE's website system. The existing site, which was custom-built for SCORE, had been running for seven years and no longer provided the capabilities needed for SCORE small business users and volunteers. It became a patchwork of fixes and changes, making the system tough for users to navigate and unable to provide reports and information on client usage and services that were needed. SCORE launched a major technical upgrade that began in August 2010. The new site launched in April 2011. With the new website, client information was not easily accessible to those who needed it, and users of the website could not always get what they were looking for. However, with the deadline looming, the site was launched anyway. Just 30 days later, the site had to be taken down because it didn't meet the needs of its users. The site did not do what it was designed to do, and everyone—staff, volunteers, and small business users—was unhappy.

For Ken this event was also troubling for him personally. The affair caused him much anxiety and frustration. He had worked tirelessly to advance SCORE and its services for the good of small business; yet, this entire process caused volunteers of the organization to react negatively. His leadership was questioned by some, and the level of confidence in Ken was diminished.

For SCORE, the incident was distressing. Sure, there was some financial loss involved because the internal and external resources used were sunk costs. But the greater loss was the loss of trust in the organization by the stakeholders—volunteers, staff, and clients alike. The organization's purpose is to make things easier for those in the field, and this situation was putting more of a burden on those that SCORE was trying to assist. Some volunteers decided to leave SCORE because of this added encumbrance.

Fortunately, Ken managed to continue in his role as the leader of SCORE and restart the website upgrade. As President Truman said, "The buck stops here," and Ken had to take ownership for the failure even though he was not a tech guy directly involved in the project. He was the leader of the organization and therefore responsible for the results of the enterprise. He held himself accountable for the failed website system.

Going forward, Ken made sure that things were done right the second time around. One of the problems of the failed website system was that there had been an inadequate analysis of SCORE's needs. "I realize now that we had bitten off more than we could chew before doing an analysis of our requirements." This time around, a proper analysis was conducted before any decisions were made. The new website reflects the collaborative effort of technicians, staff, and volunteers to get things right. IT people consulted with staff and volunteers at every turn. Ultimately, SCORE chose a better platform for the website system at a fraction of what the failed website had cost.

Beyond the website, the experience "changed everything"—the way SCORE assesses risk, the way it vets new ideas, and the way it listens to staff and volunteers. Few would characterize the experience as a good thing, but great lessons came out of it, and ultimately, the organization will be in a better place.

Ken says he's still working to regain the lost trust and confidence that he (and SCORE) had enjoyed before the failed website. "I'm working diligently to ensure that the staff and our volunteers trust me to make good decisions in the future. I'm doing this in an open environment, sharing the pending decisions with our stakeholders." The new website (the same URL of www.score.org) supports SCORE offerings for current and would-be small-business owners and entrepreneurs, including free mentoring (in person or via email); live and recorded webinars; tools, templates, resources, and tips; and local workshop information.

Ken's Lessons

- *Take the time to do proper analysis for any pending change.* The old adage of "haste makes waste" is displayed in the results of the rush to upgrade the website without taking the time to do a complete analysis of SCORE's needs. Much of the time, effort, and cost put in to the first release of the site were a waste, but there were lessons learned.

- *Collaboration creates trust.* The lack of collaboration in the initial website project resulted in a product that didn't suit anyone. It destroyed the confidence that many people had in Ken and in SCORE. By collaborating on the new website, there were no secrets; everyone had an opportunity to give input. Everyone felt vested in the results.

- *Delegation doesn't obviate supervision.* It's often said that a good executive knows how to delegate, and that's true. But delegating responsibility for a project doesn't eliminate the need for a business owner to fully understand a project's parameters and to supervise what's going on. Ultimately, it is the business owner who is responsible for *everything* that happens in a business, so he or she should certainly be involved to some extent in all of the business' activities.

I had a similar IT disaster several years ago. I had started my first website in 1997. About five years later, I decided that continual patches to the site were no longer the answer—I needed a complete upgrade. At that time, I happened to meet with a successful marketing person and began to discuss my website with him. In his opinion, I really needed two websites—one exclusively for my newsletter, Big Ideas for Small Businesses (which was a print product at that time), and one for Barbara Weltman. In his view, these were two separate brands, and having a single website confused the issues. Two sites would allow, he said, for separate conversations online with viewers and unique marketing opportunities for each site. Since I'm no marketing expert, I thought about this suggestion and decided at the time he was right. I engaged a new IT firm to create two websites for me. When I was all done, I had spent about $15,000 on the new sites, (a lot of money for me back in 2002) and each site linked to the other.

Having two websites instead of one was a serious mistake for me. The marketing opportunities never developed. Having two sites diluted my brand and created duplicative work on each site. And, of course, there was the extra money it cost to maintain two sites instead of one. Because of the investment in both sites, it was a difficult decision to abandon one, but I had to do it. At considerable additional cost, I returned to a single site and blended all of my activities under this banner.

Barbara's Lessons

- *Don't listen to the experts when your gut says otherwise—* or at least get a second opinion. I was unduly impressed by the credentials of the person who steered me in the wrong direction. My gut told me that a single site, with separate pages, would accomplish my goals, but I didn't listen to myself.

- *Don't be dazzled by credentials.* Today, there are so many people calling themselves small-business experts, but how many of them are truly deserving of the "expert" label? This marketing person appeared to know what he was saying because his firm had had success. That fact, alone, should not be the determining factor in whether to listen to someone who claims to know what's right. While I respect experts, I learned from this experience to be wary of their opinions without doing my own research.

Ken Yancey

CEO of SCORE for the past 25 years, Ken started his career as a banker in Houston, Texas. When he was laid off from one bank, he left banking to work for a former customer of his, running this customer's various branches. Later he went to work for a nonprofit  organization and eventually found his way to SCORE which is headquartered in Henderson, Virginia.

Lesson

Be Prepared to Adapt

Joel Libava

The Franchise King®

> *"Adapt or perish, now as ever, is nature's inexorable imperative."*
>
> —H.G. Wells

Bob Dylan's "Times they are a changin'" wasn't a statement only about the 60s; the message is eternal. Nothing stays the same forever. It fact, the message of change has become more acute as technology, world events, and other dramatic upheavals usher in change with greater rapidity.

One of the biggest advantages for small businesses is the ability to make decisions swiftly and take action immediately in order to adapt to change. Unlike large companies that have committees, procedures, and bureaucracy, owners in small businesses can identify the need to make changes and then act. If a business needs to buy tablets for staff members, the owner looks at the company's financials to see how this can be done. Usually, if the need is pressing enough, the owner will make it happen. In contrast, large organizations study the need and incorporate any purchasing decisions into its longrange plans, which can result in delaying an acquisition such as this for some time.

Unfortunately, not everyone or every business is good at handling change. The impact of intransigence can be devastating. At least that's the experience of Joel Libava. Joel was willing to change—the people he was working with weren't. Joel Libava became a franchise broker when he was downsized from a management position in an automobile franchise in 2001. Joining his father in a business that took its marching orders from a franchise brokerage group to which they were connected, he quickly learned the business and found that he really liked it. He went into his community, the

Cleveland area, with networking, speaking, and eventually with blogging (he actually started the first-ever blog solely focused on franchising.) to make the connections he needed for his business, which was matching people with franchise opportunities.

Then the Internet changed everything in his business. The brokerage group that he was with started to charge him for Internet "leads." A lead was the name, address, phone number, and email address of someone who was presumably interested in buying a franchise. Eventually, these leads, which Joel called, "inquires," because they were of extremely low quality, were offered to other brokers around the country. That's because Joel refused to pay for more than his budget allowed for. It was pretty aggravating to Joel, especially since some of the leads were from his own backyard. He certainly didn't want to see someone in Cleveland get matched to a franchise by someone in Atlanta or San Diego. Joel and his Dad paid for their territory, and it was supposed to be protected. In other words, brokers from other areas of the country couldn't work with people in Joel's geographical area.

However, the brokerage group pretty much ignored the arrangement and allowed others to call on prospective franchise owners in his territory. The group had made that change, among others, and they would not deviate from it— no matter what.

At first, Joel tried to make changes to the situation from within. At the group's conventions, he voiced his objections to the new strategy of the brokerage group. His complaints were never addressed to his satisfaction. The brokerage group at that time was experiencing a lot of inner turmoil . . . which eventually led to the founder being bought out in what Joel felt was an underhanded way by a small group of existing franchise brokers.

Joel was at a crossroads; he was seriously dissatisfied with the ways things stood because of the new reality created by the Internet and by the group he was a part of. He saw his choices as adapt, or ultimately, fail. He chose to adapt. Over the course of about two years, he made a dramatic change in his business model. In 2006, he began to blog about franchising at a time when blogging was new. He was quickly establishing himself as one of the top franchise experts in the country. During this time, his dad got really sick and died of lung cancer. Joel left the brokerage group and chose to go out on his own. Before his father passed, he spoke with him about his plans to leave, and his dad told him to just do it. He became an independent franchise broker—quite a rare bird at the time. He struggled for a couple of years. One of the reasons he struggled was that a huge number of new brokers were suddenly appearing on the scene. All of a sudden he found himself competing with people that had no idea what they were doing. The other reason? The 2008 recession. Very few people were willing to risk their money on a business— even a franchise business—because of worries about the economy. It was a tough period. It was also when Joel decided to not be a broker anymore.

Joel became an advisor rather than a broker. He used all of the new social media tools, including Facebook and Twitter, to put himself out there as a franchise expert. He became the *"Franchise Expert in Residence"* for the Small Business Trends website, one of the most highly-trafficked sites in small business. He was asked to write for several other small business websites as well. He was everywhere—and still is. He was approached by the Small Business Administration's marketing firm to write franchise-specific articles for their young SBA blog. He ended up helping put together the team of small business experts that contribute monthly columns there. Then, an editor at Wiley Publishing (which happens to be the publisher of a number of my books) contacted him about writing a much-needed book on franchise ownership. He wrote the book, and it was released at the end of December 2011. It's called *Become a Franchise Owner!: The Start-Up Guide To Lowering Risk, Making Money, and Owning What you Do*. It has done very well on Amazon.com, and Joel still gets calls and emails from people who have read it. In effect, he has become the go-to guy in franchising for several national media outlets. Joel continues to expand his visibility in the small-business community and remains optimistic about the future of franchising and his role in it. He told me that he's "trying to change the franchise world." Joel is focused on informing today's would-be franchise owners about the pros and cons of franchise business ownership and teaching them how to do great research. He wants people to understand that while franchising is a great business model, it's not perfect. He told me that "People fail. Franchisors lie. Stuff just happens, sometimes. I want to make sure that people looking into franchise ownership go into it with their eyes wide open."

The small business world needs more people like Joel Libava.

Joel's Lessons

- *Nothing changes if nothing changes.* In order to make improvements to a business, things have to change. Changes can be gradual or dynamic, small or great. But change must happen for things to change.

- *Don't stay in a situation that's aggravating, unrewarding, or unsatisfying; make a change.* Change can be scary because whatever is new is unfamiliar. However, when you come to the realization that life's too short to settle for a bad situation, change is the only option. In business, if something isn't working, change is imperative. You can't continue to sell an item that the public has no interest in. You can't retain an employee who isn't doing her job, even if she's been with the company for a long time.

I confess that I'm a creature of habit. I love routine and believe it has served me well over the years. It's given me structure that's allowed me to accomplish a lot of work each day. Just to give you an idea about a day in the life of Barbara, I rise early (usually before six) without an alarm, usually go to the club to do weight training, and then walk a few miles. After showering, I'm at my computer checking for tax news (I have half a dozen sources I peruse each day.). Then I check emails, and I begin my work day, addressing projects according to deadlines. Occasionally, I'll have a meeting or event to attend. Frequently I'll be speaking with reporters or fielding phone calls from people seeking business information or advice. It's a good routine, but every day is different, the unexpected (good or bad) always happens, and the routine is rewarding for me.

But within this routine, there have been many dramatic changes that I've had to adapt to as a result of technology. When I started on my own in 1983, there were no computers, no Internet, no overnight delivery everywhere, and no email. I had to type on an electric typewriter (the automatic correction feature with the white tape seemed very advanced). I had to go to the library to do research. I had to send articles by snail mail (that's all there was to many locations at that time). Long-distance phone calls cost extra. Does anyone besides me remember carbon paper? Well, things have certainly changed. In 1984, I got my first computer and a continuous form paper printer (remember the sprockets?). Two years later, I had a fax machine. The Internet came into its own in the mid-1990s, but access via dial-up was slow, and sites were limited. I launched my first website in 1997 and switched to broadband as soon as it was available in my area. It took me a while before I began to use a smartphone, but now I go everywhere with my iPad. And there are certain apps that I can't imagine ever being without.

What am I trying to say about technology? It's keep up or fail, which means adapting to the new business landscape—there is no other option. And there's more to learn. It's not merely a question of how to use the technology itself; it's also how it's being used in business and the changes in social mores that are happening as a result. Communicating today isn't as simple as picking up a landline and making a call. Some business people don't even have a landline anymore. Many prefer to get messages by email or texting.

Adapting to the latest technology isn't easy for everyone, especially boomers like me who grew up with black-and-white TV. But adapting, with the help of experts (or your children or grandchildren who know no other way to function), has many rewards. Technologies can save time. They certainly save money, enabling you for example to email invoices rather than sending them with postage stamps—or, even better, swiping credit cards on the spot for instant payment. And they can open up vistas that we previously never dreamed up, such as doing business across the globe.

Barbara's Lessons

- *Adapt to the latest technologies.* This means making both a financial investment in new equipment or options (e.g., embracing cloud solutions) and a time commitment to learning how to use the technologies.

- *Stay current in business thinking.* Technology isn't the only field that you should pay attention to when it comes to change. How are you communicating with those in generations other than yours, which may require some adaptation on your part? Millennials work differently than boomers or GenXers, and here comes Gen Z. What are futurists saying about developments of interest? This information can impact what you offer and how you market it.

Joel Libava

Owner of Franchise Selection Specialists Inc., Joel Libava, The Franchise King®, is a top franchise expert who teaches and coaches people on how to choose, research, and buy a franchise. He's the author of several eBooks as well as *Become a Franchise Owner!* He's written over 1,600 articles on franchising, small business, and innovation. He's a regular contributor to SBA.gov and Small Business Trends and occasionally writes for Entrepreneur.com, Bplans.com, and, most recently, *The New York Times.* https://www.thefranchiseking.com.

Lesson

Know How Your Customers Buy

Robert Levin

Founder of the New York Enterprise Report

> *"The more you engage with customers the clearer things become and the easier it is to determine what you should be doing."*
>
> —John Russell, President of Harley Davidson

The problem with many entrepreneurs who have a great idea for a product or service is believing the line from the movie *Field of Dreams:* "If you build it, they will come." These entrepreneurs think that launching a business with a great product or service is all that's needed for success. Unfortunately, start-up enthusiasm often overtakes good sense to step back and take the time to do things right from the start. It's not enough to have a *good* idea; it has to be the *right* idea. This means that the product or service is what customers actually want, and you know how to sell it to them. It's all too easy to pour money and spend a lot of time and effort trying to foist an idea on customers who aren't interested. That's what happened to Rob Levin, who failed to understand how his customers bought at the inception of his business.

In 2003, Robert formed RSL Media LLC, a media company providing knowledge and inspiration from renowned experts to small businesses in the New York City area. The printing of its monthly magazine, *New York Enterprise Report,* began in the spring of 2004. The magazine was free to readers whether in print or online; revenue was dependent entirely on advertising. Circulation quickly reached 10,000, which is not bad for a new publication. However, advertisers weren't signing up as quickly as subscribers, and Rob was burning through money at an alarming rate.

Rob was under the working assumption that if he created a great magazine (which he did—business owners loved it), advertisers would line up to buy ads and "get in front of his audience." So, before the magazine's launch and shortly thereafter, he spent all of his time working on the editorial of the magazine and no time speaking with potential advertisers. After the launch, he met with what he thought were potential advertisers, but his sales efforts fell flat. He became very frustrated...Truth was, Rob, despite his experience, made some classic mistakes. He didn't really understand who his advertisers were likely to be, and he didn't know how they bought advertising.

He was confident that he could figure it out. After all, he'd previously been a CEO of another publication, and he knew he really had something special with *New York Enterprise Report*. But it took him nearly three years to start making things better. In 2006, he hired his first fulltime sales person, something that in retrospect he should have done from the outset. He took a sales training course to learn how to make the sales process work for him, and he focused on what his customers wanted. Things started to turn around.

He learned that he had two groups of customers: subscribers and advertisers. He had no difficulty pleasing subscribers—they loved the information they got from the magazine, as it helped save them money and run their businesses better (I was a contributor to the publication). He eventually learned how to please his other group of customers—advertisers and partners—the revenue generators. By listening to what this group had to say, he found out that his inability to sell them wasn't because the magazine was lacking in any way; it was simply because of low circulation. His pool of advertisers, which are mainly Fortune 500 and other large companies, weren't interested in putting their money into a product that drew a small audience. So Rob focused on raising circulation, and it quickly rose by 33,000—now he had a readership of over 100,000. He also learned to better identify potential customers so he could spend his time selling to them rather than wasting it on prospects that would never become customers.

Throughout its existence, the *New York Enterprise Report* was a fixture in New York City, hosting numerous business events including the prestigious Small Business Awards and the Best Accountants and Attorneys in the Tri-State Area. Annually, it also recognized the 10 Great Entrepreneurial Places to Work For. It hosted seminars and webinars to keep readers up-to-date on key issues impacting their businesses. His company partnered with the likes of Con Edison, Time Warner Cable Business Class, and Citibank, among others. The *New York Enterprise Report* has since been sold and Robert Levin continues today as chief SMB Officer of RSL Media and editor-in-chief of SpeakSMB.

Rob's Lessons

- *Meet with potential customers before starting a business and ask the right questions:* What do you want? What would you pay for it? Why would you not buy it? This simple action will help you determine if people want what you have to sell, what to price it at, and what not to do that would turn customers off.

- *Don't ignore opportunity costs.* Rob's failure to more quickly address his problem caused him to miss out on the tail end of a great publication era. This cost him a lot more in lost revenue than it would have cost him in hiring the right sales people to help him.

- *Don't let confidence trump knowledge.* It's great, and in fact essential, for a business owner to have confidence in him/herself and the business offering. But confidence by itself won't overcome problems. These problems need to be addressed; and, in order to do this, you need to learn what the real problems are. Rob had enough confidence; he just initially lacked understanding of what his customers wanted.

I also experienced the exact same failure as Rob in not understanding what my customers wanted. Like Rob, I had two groups of customers for my radio show: listeners and advertisers. But unlike Rob, I was slower to understand the shortcomings of my assumptions when it came to one group. Let me give you some background about the show. In January 2008, BizFilings, a large national company that offers online incorporations and provides other services for small businesses, asked me to co-host a radio show. I'd worked with them before, providing content for their site, and we had a great relationship. We called the show *Build Your Business*. The show aired live on the Internet, with segments stored so that listeners who could not hear the show in real time could do so via iTunes, through wsradio. com, and in other ways. We had no trouble getting top guests, including Steve Forbes, Fran Tarkenton, Michael Gerber, Rep. Sam Graves (head of the House's Small Business Committee), Karen Mills (then head of the SBA), Ken Yancey (head of SCORE), and, yes, Rob Levin. After just five months, BizFilings wanted to pursue a different course, leaving me with the show. There was a monthly charge by the station to run the show, which had been paid by BizFilings; as a great gesture to me, they paid through the end of the year. After that, it was up to me to find advertisers to defray the production cost and, hopefully, make the show profitable. That never happened.

I believed, wrongly, that if I worked harder at pursuing sponsors, I'd get them. I didn't understand how radio advertising worked. Rob figured out his problem in three years; it took me five. What I eventually learned was that advertisers want repetition, and my show couldn't provide it. The show was one hour weekly, but advertisers wanted a daily show so that their ads could be repeated every day. No matter how great the show's content—and it was great—or how many listeners I had—and the numbers were good—the advertisers weren't interested because it didn't meet their needs.

I loved doing the show because of the fabulous people I got to interview and the knowledge I gained from them. Having a radio show was also a great calling card; include a mention of it in a 30-second self-introduction, and people become hooked and want to know more. But it was a big time commitment for no financial return. My failure was not understanding what my customers wanted. Once I learned that I was never ever going to get advertisers, I had to drop the show (although I continued with a monthly show for fun for several more years).

Barbara's Lessons

- *If things aren't working as planned, don't delay in finding out the problem.* I initially tried to get advertisers on my own—something I knew nothing about. Eventually I spoke with media experts and learned about radio advertising. This was something I should have done much sooner.

- *Set business priorities.* Enjoying something that's losing money isn't good business sense. I loved having the radio show and the connection to awesome experts. But a business isn't a hobby to pass the time; it must be profitable to warrant your time and financial commitment.

Robert Levin

Rob, a CPA by trade, has expanded his entrepreneurial endeavors beyond his highly successful and well-respected *New York Enterprise Report* to provide marketing guidance for small and mid-sized businesses selling to business through SpeakSMB.

https://www.speaksmb.com/

Lesson

Listen to Good Advice

Brian Moran

Brian Moran & Associates

> *"Many receive advice, only the wise profit from it."*
>
> —Harper Lee, author of
> *To Kill a Mockingbird*

The very characteristics that make a good entrepreneur can also lead to his undoing: intelligence, bravery, independence, and perseverance. We know our business better than anyone else? Notice the question mark. It's there to raise the question: Do we really know our business better than an outsider? Sometimes yes, but sometimes no. The savvy entrepreneur knows when to heed sage advice. Unfortunately, it's not always easy to determine whether advice is sound and should be followed.

That was the dilemma that Brian Moran found himself in when the economy hit the fan in 2007. He started a printing business, Moran Media Group, in 2003, doing contract publishing for some major organizations, including the U.S. Small Business Administration, Junior Chamber International (JCI), and the Edward Lowe Foundation. These contract publications weren't sold to the general public; they were distributed by the organizations for which they were printed. Brian's revenues came from advertisers who knew the value of appearing in these publications. Business was booming, and he even received a buyout offer from a private equity firm.

But in the heady days that preceded the Great Recession, Brian thought he could do better and grow his business. He neglected the contract publishing work in favor of starting his own magazines, including *Urban Success* and *Winning Bids*. He also added a website, SmallBusinessEdge.com, that he hoped would become a go-to destination for small-business owners and would-be entrepreneurs seeking information and advice.

Then the handwriting appeared on the wall: Advertising in his publications began to slide dramatically. It's commonly accepted wisdom that you can foretell a recession by looking at declines in advertising revenue. A drop in advertising revenues usually precedes a recession by about six months.

The signs were there, but Brian refused to see them. Instead, he ploughed ahead, putting more money into the website and focusing on his own print products. At this time, Brian was working with a business coach who advised him to ride out the recession storm with contract publishing, which was a solid money-making activity. Advertisers were still willing to pay for placements in the contract publications of the SBA and other large organizations. Brian didn't listen to this advice, and his company became a victim of the economy.

Brian didn't listen because he thought he knew better and could ride out the recession without making changes in his business. He had a lot invested—in terms of ego, time, and money—in his vision for his company. He thought that by sticking with it, he could succeed. He obviously hadn't seen the cartoon by Randy Glasbergen. In it, a little boy with an incorrect answer to an addition problem on a blackboard talks to his teacher. The caption said: *"My dad says persistence is the key to success. So I'm going to keep giving you the same wrong answer until it becomes the right answer."*

Persistence isn't the only reason Brian didn't listen to the advice of his coach. He just didn't appreciate the fact that sometimes an outsider can step back and view the picture calmly and rationally with nothing invested and can see better than someone intimately familiar with the situation.

For Brian, this failure was life-changing. Soon he became exhausted from trying to save a dying business in a horrible economy. He needed a time-out to get back into shape and fortunately, found it by becoming the Executive Director of Sales Development with The Wall Street Journal at the end of 2010. In this role, Brian had the opportunity to meet great people, work on interesting projects, and (most importantly) catch his breath so he could once again pursue his entrepreneurial dreams.

After 18 months on the job, he was ready and able to start Brian Moran Associates. Since July 2012, he has been re-connecting with the small business community through his new business model. Rather than putting all his eggs in the publishing basket as he had formerly done, he now relies on a three-basket approach. He's paid on retainer for consulting work, he pursues special projects that generate fixed payments, and he undertakes some performance-based work in which he receives a percentage of the funds he generates for clients. His business is once again booming.

Brian now solicits advice from a newly formed board of advisors. This time around, he is heeding the advice he's been given. He's also more cautious about making changes when things are going well. Brian only takes calculated risks and carefully monitors expenses so that he won't experience the same failure again.

Brian's Lessons

- *Find a good business coach or put together a board of advisors for your company.* Getting an outsider's perspective can be invaluable.
- *Diversify your revenue streams.* Instead of concentrating on a single revenue stream, which could dry up at any moment, develop multiple channels of bringing in income for your business.

There's a bit of Hebrew wisdom from *The Teachings of the Fathers:* "Find yourself a teacher and get yourself a friend." Scholars have interpreted this to mean that a teacher will challenge your answers, and a friend will challenge your questions. When teacher and friend are embodied in the same person, wow!

Brian found a trusted teacher and friend in his business coach, but failed to follow the good advice that he received. He just didn't listen. I had the opposite experience. I heeded bad advice from someone who was neither my teacher nor my friend, and it cost me dearly.

Years ago, before the dot-com bubble when the Internet was young and websites were still a novelty, I recognized the value of having an online presence and started a website. Back then, my company was BWideas. com, and the website used this name as its URL. But like many others at that time, I had no idea how to monetize the website. A successful business owner who I knew locally had a vision for me. He suggested that I split the site into two sites to better identify my offerings for viewers' needs: one site focused on promoting me (BarbaraWeltman.com), and the other (BWideas. com) was content rich, providing information for small business owners. He made a compelling case about how viewers were confused by a single site and how two sites were better than one. I accepted this advice and followed up on it. I spent more than $10,000 developing and maintaining the two sites. This was a lot of money for me at the time, and it took a while to recoup from this failed endeavor. After several years of burning money and duplicating my efforts, I regrouped and returned to a single site. It meant yet another investment in site development, but I felt a whole lot better about the creation of a single, new site. It was more reflective of me and what I was trying to do with content for the small business community.

It's great to have a teacher and receive advice. It's quite another thing to discern whether the person giving the advice really knows what he or she is talking about so you can decide whether it's worthy of being followed. The visions of the person I listened to were wrong for me, and the suggestion of having two sites was wrong. Luckily I was able to correct my mistake in listening to him.

Barbara's Lessons

- *Be open to outsiders' opinions, but recognize the interests of the person giving advice to you.* The intentions may be sincere, but come from a perspective that does not align with yours. Not all advice is good advice.

- *Objectively evaluate the advice, but don't hesitate to reassess.* Just because you follow good advice doesn't mean it's the best advice for your situation. Continually question, examine, and assess how things are going so you can limit the time and money you put into activities that won't pay off.

Brian Moran

Brian is the head of Brian Moran and Associates, a consulting company in the greater New York City area that helps small business owners nationwide manage and grow their businesses. He blogs about small business issues for American Express  OPEN Forum and other outlets and co-authored *Lessons from the Great Recession*. www.smallbusinessedge.com.

Conclusion

Student for Life

"Make failure your teacher, not your undertaker."
—Zig Zigler

If you're going to strive for success, you're bound to make mistakes. Maybe you are rushed, overzealous, or uninformed about something (but think you know about it). Whatever the reason for errors, accept the fact that they will happen and don't be regretful or down on yourself. Making mistakes should be something that's prized, not feared. As the stories in this book have shown, highly successful people make mistakes all the time. Some failures are big, some are even bigger, but none need result in the end of your dreams to achieve.

Writing this book has made me realize that I'm a student for life. I expect to continue working *to make entrepreneurs smarter* (the mantra for my business) through the activities at BigIdeasForSmallBusiness.com. In the process, I now fully anticipate making mistakes and having failures. I embrace these missteps and plan to learn valuable lessons from them that I hope to pass on to you.

If you have experienced failures in your business activities and you'd like to share them publicly, I would appreciate hearing from you at Barbara@BigIdeasForSmallBusiness.com. Your experiences can be valuable lessons to other entrepreneurs.

Looking ahead, I will continue my exploration of failure, focusing on people outside the business world. Many figures in entertainment, sports, government, and other arenas have also had failures from which they recovered from, only to be stronger and wiser. Their failures are your lessons on what not to do so you can succeed in your endeavors.